Life and Death

—— IN THE ——

Battle of Britain

Published by IWM, Lambeth Road, London SE1 6HZ
iwm.org.uk

ISBN 978-1-904897-31-6

A catalogue record for this book is available from the British Library

Designed by Adrian Hunt
Printed and bound by CPI Group (UK) Ltd, Croydon, CR0 4YY

Pages 2, 8, 24, 129, 133 and 135 courtesy of Piers Mayfield

PREVIOUS PAGE: Guy Mayfield (right), with Peter Watson (left) and
19 Squadron's adjutant H Nicholls

FRONT COVER: (composite), © IWM CH 1366 (detail, this image
has been artificially coloured), © IWM CH 6381 (detail), © IWM CH
7688 (detail)

BACK COVER: Courtesy of Piers Mayfield

10 9 8 7 6 5 4 3 2 1

Contents

Foreword

PIERS MAYFIELD

My FATHER wrote a lot. In the 1930s he worked at the *Guardian*, not the daily newspaper, which in those days was the *Manchester Guardian*, but one associated with the Church of England. This likely made it relatively easy for him to get into the habit of keeping a diary about what he was doing at Duxford. The first two entries, those for 12 December 1939 and 21 January 1940, suggest someone who was used to writing about the world around him, a skill which had played a big part in his life for several years. At times during the Battle of Britain and later, this may have helped him to feel that the world had not gone completely mad.

I'm not aware that he kept a diary earlier in his life, and he certainly did not do so after the war when he was so busy with other writings. Apart from his administrative work as the Archdeacon of Hastings and the regular production of sermons, between 1958 and 1966 he published three books. For recreation he took to oil painting. Wherever we lived he would occupy a big room, one half of which was full of what he needed for writing and the other with an easel, together with all the mess which oil painters seem to need and with a radio on which he listened to Radio Luxembourg while he daubed.

In 1964 he began typing up the diary which he'd kept at Duxford in 1940 and 1941, handwritten in blue RAF-issue notebooks, of which I have some of the originals. He wanted to leave a legible version of this for posterity and, as he was probably aware that his handwriting, although big, bold and usually black, could sometimes be a bit of a scrawl which was difficult to read, he typed the records up with a view to sending it off to the Imperial War Museum. Understandably, as he was picking out the letters, memories and reflections occurred to him – afterthoughts which he hand-wrote in the margin of the typed copy, making a bit of a mess of what he was trying to render beautiful.

When I was small I loved the stories Guy told at mealtimes; naturally, as I grew older, I wondered how much of them was fantasy and how much reality, proportions which only he knew. Perhaps he hoped to produce something which gave more space for his storytelling when he retired. His additions gave the impression that, if he had had the time, he might have liked to write a memoir of his experiences at Duxford. Unfortunately, in his last years as Archdeacon he was not well and he died at the age of seventy-one.

Before he died he asked Thelma, my mother, if she would type a copy of what he'd got together and see if the Imperial War Museum was interested. She said she would, although she hated thinking about the war and never spoke about it. Born in 1908, she was the daughter of an Engineer Captain in the Royal Navy, Malcolm Johnson; so, during the First World War, she will have been old enough to be bothered by what her father was having to do and what might happen to him. She spent the Second World War at Linton, within ten miles of Duxford, with my elder brother Robert, born in August 1940 at the height of the Battle of Britain and, from September 1942, me – the pair of us providing her with too much opportunity to worry about the consequences if the war was lost.

By 1945, having spent at least nine years of her life dreading what might happen to her nearest and dearest, she wanted nothing more to do with war. Typing up the Duxford diary would also have been particularly painful because she knew a number of the pilots whose lives and deaths Guy records, so she asked me if I would carry out his wishes.

As I sat typing, I thought of the ashtray before him on the desk at which he worked. The ashtray, I long ago decided, must have come from Duxford. Ideal for a pipe-smoker like Guy, it was metal, heavy, round and a good nine inches across, with grooves around the edge upon which pipes could be rested and with plenty of space in the centre for ash. It looked as if it had originally been part of the engine of a Spitfire, which some thoughtful RAF engineer had mounted on wood so that it would not scratch the top of the padre's table while he was writing his diary and puffing away as he did so. I don't know for sure because, like Thelma, Guy never talked about the war. Like the war, the ashtray was simply there, never to be discussed – a silence which made discovering what happened to him at Duxford so moving.

Guy Mayfield outside No. 19 Squadron's hangar, RAF Duxford. Today this building contains an exhibition about the Battle of Britain, but in 1940 it was one of the many locations Guy visited to talk to the airmen as they worked.

Introduction

CARL WARNER

GUY MAYFIELD, so lovingly described by Piers in his foreword, arrived at RAF Duxford on 2 February 1940. This placed him at the centre of a community of men and women who were about to take part in the greatest defensive air battle ever fought. In the pages of his diary we find one of the finest accounts of a fighter station at war. It is full of insight into the mind of a man who made an enormous, unsung contribution to victory, and into those of others on the station whose mental, physical and spiritual well-being he cared about so deeply.

By 1940 Duxford had already been operational for over twenty years, and was home to many fighter squadrons and test units. Guy most often references Nos. 19 and 66, who were both already there when he arrived, but they were soon joined by others, including several units that would form part of the famous 'Duxford Wing'. Its aircraft and men were detached to operate over the North Sea and over the Channel, notably during the evacuation of Dunkirk. Then, in June 1940, the daily grind of the Battle of Britain-proper took over. Once the Battle ended, RAF Fighter Command went on the attack, launching 'sweeps' over northern France. Duxford's pilots were involved, too, and at great cost, as the 1941 pages of the diary reveal.

Much has been written of Duxford's role in this defining conflict, but there are few accounts as honest, open and revealing as this. It is not a varnished or airbrushed tale. The immediacy of the format, combined with the extra commentary that Guy supplied later as he reflected on his wartime impressions (set in italics within brackets throughout), reveals the men and women of Duxford in 1940 to be very human indeed: real people operating under huge amounts of pressure. It is the story of Duxford's war but it was undoubtedly replicated, if rarely documented with such skill, across the UK in the summer of 1940. This alone makes it extraordinarily valuable.

Keeping track of the names that pass through his life is difficult. Guy introduces a huge cast of characters, many of whom he refers to by nickname only. I have included what photographs we have where I could. Some of these men went on to huge success in other fields: 'Dr Applee' (John Apley), for example, one of Duxford's Medical Officers, became one of the world's foremost paediatricians and a medical writer of much renown. Ian Little, with whom Guy enjoys many late-night conversations, became a Professor of Development Economics at Oxford. Other careers did not proceed as planned: 'F L Trewella', the hapless chaplain who Guy is rather despairingly forced to send away from the station after a series of faux pas, is likely Frank Lionel Trewella. His records reveal that by 1942 he had left the RAF, thus confirming Guy's suspicion that he was not really cut out for life as a service chaplain.

There will remain, though, some people who go unrecorded in other sources, and musings that are still open to interpretation, as we would expect from such a deeply personal account. We may, for example, wonder why, other than his tragic misfortune and early death, Guy described Pilot Officer Dini ('Dimmy' in the text), in his 6 June 1940 entry, as having 'lived an unlovely life'.

Chaplains – 'padres' to many – were an important part of the makeup of the armed forces. As squadron leaders, RAF chaplains were, in terms of the 'stripes on their sleeves', relatively senior. The Reverend H D L Veiner, the man tasked with forming the Chaplains Department for the RAF in 1918, wrote, 'Whether uniform is a hindrance or not depends upon the type of man who wears it, and how he wears it.' Guy's seniority, as we will see, was no barrier to his effectiveness as a counsellor, friend and mentor.

Guy was thrust into what, to many of us, would appear to be an almost impossibly complex, wide-ranging and ever-expanding job. His was a life full of official and unofficial duties that had to be navigated with sensitivity and discretion: 'Work on the plans for the new mortuary. Fussing as Mess officer. More attempts to get a pension for Wilson's mother. Many letters,' pithily describes one afternoon, for example.

This job brought him into contact with all ranks at Duxford – from the Station Commander to the most junior airman. All could, and often did, ask for his help over tricky issues that lay outside the chain of command, where answers could not easily be found in King's Regulations or Air Ministry Orders. 'Woody' Woodhall, Duxford's Station Commander during the Battle, set the tone, as Mayfield recalled on 13 March 1940: 'Soon after his arrival he sent for me and talked about the morale and discipline of the pilots. I was to get them to bed earlier. I was to see that they drank less. To this one, I asked him, "But how, sir?" "By drinking with them yourself and setting an example."'

Drinking is a thread that runs through the diary. Most of the pilots – indeed, most of the officers with whom Guy mixed – were heavy drinkers, consuming what today would be considered terrifying amounts of alcohol, and mixing it with the daily operation of what were then the most potent and technologically advanced weapons available. On more than one occasion Guy dealt with the aftermath of a drunken party, clearing up both literally and metaphorically the detritus of a wild night. He often deftly managed the 'morning after', with pilots regretful of their inebriated belligerence, and who required a delicate 'talking to'. Sometimes, it was the more prosaic handling of the physical consequences of huge alcohol consumption that needed his skills.

His judgement was often called upon to help with personnel issues. The squadron commanders, responsible for leading their pilots into battle in the air, occasionally asked him to judge their 'morale'. 'Morale' in this case was a sensitive euphemism for 'fitness for combat'. It is hard not to sympathise with everyone in this situation. First, the squadron leaders, little older than the pilots they commanded, who in the brutal world of dog-fighting had to be able to rely on the skills and temperament of their squadron-mates: there was no room for sentimentality. Second, the pilots themselves: men trying to do their jobs, who sometimes, through no fault of their own, did not have the peculiar skillset of the natural fighter ace. Third, Guy: thrust into this delicate dynamic. It is a measure of his discretion that he remained trusted by them all, and it is not difficult to imagine a hundred such conversations being had throughout the RAF at this time.

It was vital that the men could trust him to act confidentially, particularly given the rules of RAF discipline. On one occasion, in April 1940, Mayfield had to quietly arrange for the transfer to non-aircraft-related duties of a member of the ground crew who he had been warned was signing off 'unfit' aircraft as safe to fly. The information came from a very junior airman, worried about what he should do given that it concerned his superior and rightly apprehensive about breaking the chain of command. Guy handled the situation with aplomb: another quiet, discreetly performed duty that, without his diary, we would never be aware of, yet one that potentially saved the life of the pilot, Francis Brinsden, who died in 1993.

The most significant task that Guy faced – and the one that is the understandable focus of his daily preoccupations and philosophical concerns – was providing a non-judgemental confidante for the young men who he knew could very well be dead by the end of the summer. Fighter pilots were by nature outwardly tough and 'devil may care' – certainly in conversations with each other. At its heart the diary is a story of the deep friendships that Guy forged with the men who felt that they could talk to him without pretence about their fears and frailties. Guy continually wrestles with the enormity of providing good counsel, and of remaining true to his faith in the face of such devastating conflict: 'All one's prayers can't keep them in the sky. It is difficult to keep the Christian hope and the faith in the little change between the two lives.'

The predictable human preoccupations of young men loom large in many of the talks. Financial and family troubles, and the inevitable and protracted talks about love and sex dominate Guy's days. Sometimes these conversations are almost unbearably poignant to a modern reader, none more so than his discussions with his closest friend, Pilot Officer Peter Watson, on 3 May 1940:

> I talked about the girl at Norwich, the gist of what I said being
> that he isn't old enough to be stable yet, and that this piece,

even from his own account, didn't sound extra hot.

He accepted it all and replied in a very depressed way: "What does it matter'? I shall be killed anyway; if not killed, I shall be maimed; there won't be much left to live with…" We talked and walked for a long time, very frankly and about many things with a directness that I never wanted to talk to any young man about. We both of us smelled death. So he feels the hurry to do things while there is time…

Peter Watson was killed less than a month later. He was 20 years old. Guy's diary entries in the days following the death of his friend are, in my opinion, some of the most moving ever written about loss.

Through all this, Guy made sure never to neglect his 'official' duties:

Felt encouraged by increase of 8 in the number of communicants. We had 15 at Easter; the usual number is about 3-5. There are a nominal 1,000 on the station, but possibly only a third are off-duty and free to come at any time. Smalley has told me not to worry about numbers: "When they hear the first big bang and mess their pants, they'll come alright."

Dealing with the business of service death – organising funerals, writing and talking to widows and grieving family members – was a vital part of his job, and again his sensitivity shines through. An entry in February 1940 is illuminating:

I took the funeral of [Pilot Officer Arthur Delamore] of 222 Sq and buried his poor bits and pieces at Whittlesford. He was a shy, elegant young man with whom no one could get on terms. He was night-flying for training and he crashed for no apparent reason. There were relatives to be written to. In the evening there was a rowdy dance in the Sergeants Mess. I didn't dance, but talked to anyone who wanted to and propped up the bar.

It is sobering to think of the men who Guy meets briefly, before the Battle of Britain begins, who do not survive the war. No. 222 Squadron's Canadian flight commander, Alvin T 'Al' Williams, whose departure Guy describes on 15 April 1940, was lost when HMS *Glorious* was sunk in April 1940. Alick Heath, whose 'morale is unjustly doubted' on Easter Day 1940, was killed flying with No. 254 Squadron in Norway. Peter King, Guy's squash partner on 25 February 1940, was killed in September of that year.

There is often a dark humour associated with some of the heartbreaking tasks he undertakes – understandably so. On one journey to talk to the wife of a missing airman, he describes 'a long, tasteless and amusing conversation on methods of how not to break the news we were bearing.'

There are many other aspects of the diary that make it worthy of repeated study, but perhaps the most important is that it reveals, through simple prose (and occasional poetry), the true heroism of many of the men and women that played their part in the Battle of Britain. It is vital to remember that in 1940 victory, at times, seemed very uncertain. The national mythology surrounding this conflict, so eloquently described by Sir Winston Churchill as an enormous debt owed by all to 'so few', is in most respects well-founded. Getting up day after day and flying and fighting, not just for their lives, but for the freedom of their (often adopted) country, with no guarantee of success, makes the people Guy describes truly inspirational. The fact that his diary reveals them to be fragile, sensitive people battling both the Luftwaffe and their own fears can only increase our admiration for this, now almost vanished, generation. It should also, I hope, increase our admiration for people such as Guy Mayfield, whose job it was to help them cope, to find peace in their combat-centred lives and, ultimately, to prevail.

Carl Warner is a curator and historian at IWM, where he has authored several exhibitions about conflict and the history of IWM's airfield branch. These include Historic Duxford, AirSpace *and the* American Air Museum.

1939

12th December

R.A.F. Cranwell. At midnight yesterday I became a chaplain R.A.F.V.R. Thelma, Bryan, my brother and I lunched at the Spanish restaurant in Swallow Street. He approved my uniform, but reminded me that the R.A.F. officers' uniform had been designed by Phyllis Dare (or was it Gladys Cooper?). He looked good as a colonel in the Guards, with the red gorgets in his lapels. They both saw me off on the 4 p.m. train to Grantham and Cranwell.

Edwards, the Assistant Chaplain-in-Chief of the R.A.F., described in his first talk to us, 30 new-fledged chaplains, what kind of war we might have to face. He didn't seem to know very much himself, but said that it was expected to become violent by the spring, and that by the summer of 1940, 40 per cent of the aircrew we should meet on our stations would be dead. The average age of R.A.F. personnel, not simply aircrew, is 23. Certainly the first impression gained in the Mess here is one of extreme youth. The pilot officers in particular look like school boys. One feels the temptation to tell them that they are staying up too late. The majority of the aircrew have yet to experience combat. Apart from reconnaissance and patrols, little else goes on in the way of operational flying beyond the pamphlet raids on Germany. What of the aircrew nerves when things hot up? How long will those who aren't killed survive mentally?

There is a lot of tension even on this station which is a training one. The pace of training is being hurried up with the result that the instructors, who are not much older than the trainees, are getting strained. One chaplain here told me that the instructors after a day's flying are too tired to do anything except sit about in the Mess and say nothing. If a pupil panics in the air, he freezes onto the controls. The instructor may, with luck, be able to use more force on his dual set of controls to overcome the panic-strength of the pupil. But if he fails, then disaster looms up. A frightened pupil forgets that there is anyone else in the aircraft besides himself. Most of the instructors have fitted mirrors so that they can see their pupils' faces and watch from their expressions whether their nerve is giving way.

My first reaction on finding 25 other newly-fledged chaplains here was to hide away, for clergy *en masse* make me shudder in any circumstances. There is nowhere to hide here. Life is public. King, who is the chaplain at Manston, told me that his reactions are similar. I felt a little more at home. There has been no just reason for my shudders. None of the clergy are parsonical; all of them, with two possible exceptions, are as unlike the ordinary run of clergy as even I could wish for. The temptation is to consider that as a collection we are not representative of the clergy. This is untrue. We are clergy with the blinds of our shop windows raised and our reserves on the way to being lifted. Another chaplain said this afternoon, "We reach a remarkably high standard", but this isn't true. The uniform seems to have a good effect on us. The common experience makes us at ease with each other.

Last night the first fatal accident for six months took place here. The pilot, who was 19, was night-flying solo and crashed on landing. He went straight into the ground; the plane exploded. Part of him was blown up and part burned. There wasn't very much left of him. We saw the flames of the crash on leaving the camp cinema. Everyone knew the cause. But no comments were made and everyone went on as if nothing had happened. There were no comments this morning in the Mess. The pilot had been with us during the day. But there was not a word of discussion, and the tragedy was treated as of no concern. It was, it might have been inferred, as normal as a safe landing. This is probably the right way to treat it all, but I would like to know what some of the trainees and instructors really think behind the mask of indifference.

I am told that every 25 miles along the coastline are small, inconspicuous buildings which contain apparatus with a ray that can put enemy magnetos out of action. The German aircraft brought down last week on the east coast, or it may have crashed, might have been destroyed by the ray. In the photos of the wreckage a small tower can be seen nearby. There was no gunfire. *(That we possessed such a ray was one form of a widespread rumour which became the more current for being allegedly highly secret. Cars were alleged to have been put out of action near Felixstowe where there was a big radar station.)*

We have had lots of services in the station chapel. The furnishings of the altar are made from parts of aircraft; the cross from the propellers, the candlesticks from cylinders and so on. It is all very ugly and very "service minded". The station chaplain, Jagoe *(who later became Chaplain-in-Chief and with whom I never got on at all well)*, puzzled many of us by praying one day "for those with whom we are at variance." Jagoe seems as fenced in by his uniform and long peace time service in the R.A.F. as we seem at sea in a new world. *(I decided that he must be committing our neighbours to God, but on asking another and more seasoned chaplain, I was assured that he was being very daring and praying for the Germans. I remembered the service I had been to a few weeks earlier in London when George Bell, the Bishop of Chichester, had prayed for the Germans, for the Nazis, openly and without evasion. He was a brave man to hold this service in London. I preferred his bravery to Jagoe's equivocation, but, I was told, there is morale to be thought of.)*

We left Cranwell on Friday and got to Grantham just in time to catch the 8.01 a.m. to Kings Cross. But the tender with our baggage was late. I was requested by the other chaplains to tell the guard to keep the train waiting till the baggage arrived as "there were 18 squadron leaders who must travel by this train". A squadron leader to the guard in this stage of the war means a bold man who leads numbers of aircraft over Germany. So the train was held up for ten minutes while the tender came. To judge by the indignant shouts, this did not please General Ironside who was in a special carriage at the rear of the train and fortunately in plain clothes. If he had been in uniform things might not have been so easy, for 18 clergymen dressed as squadron leaders would not equal a general in full regalia.

I went straight to R.A.F. Uxbridge to which Edwards, Assistant Chaplain-in-Chief, had posted me as supernumerary so that I could work under him at the Air Ministry. No sooner had I reported and signed the book, than the adjutant told me that I could not be accommodated on the station nor could I live out at Esher. I put the dilemma to him. There was nowhere for me to live on the station and anyway I didn't want to live there, and yet I was not allowed to leave the station. I suggested that I should sleep in the open in my anti-gas overall. But this got us nowhere at all. I became obstinate and eventually pulled the senior station chaplain away from lunch. He certainly didn't want a new boy on his station and he wanted to finish his lunch. We approached the Group Captain who wanted peace. I was set free and told not to appear again till I was posted away. Moral: if everything is not put in writing in the service, there is confusion. It was Edwards' fault. He had never sent a signal to explain why I came.

1940

21st January 1940

I am still living at home at Esher. In one sense life hasn't changed very much. I still catch the same train to London every day though now I wear a splendid uniform (everything depends on the R.A.F., it is thought) and go to the Air Ministry in Kingsway and not to the *Guardian* office. I have had a medical examination rather late in time. I was congratulated on my splendid two front teeth but I felt obliged to point out that they are not mine but false ones. I wonder if many R.A.F. doctors are like the Wing Commander ones at the Air Ministry. I was laid up with "flu" last week; otherwise I should have gone to a station. I have been usefully employed and learned a lot. Edwards, who can't spell or construct a simple sentence, has tried to write some notes for the guidance of us, new boys. I have done the job for him with, I hope, some tact. I've rewritten everything he wrote, and made excuses for drastic revision: "You see, sir, I don't think those of us who have no experience of the service would quite realise" etc. I have also checked the postings of all the chaplains in the service. This information has been put by Edwards on a venetian blind hanging on the wall. At night it must be pulled up in case a spy should lower himself from the roof and take a photo of it and thus see where the more sizeable R.A.F. units are. *(When I suggested that a card index would be safer and simpler, he was puzzled. "Why?" he asked. I remembered my hopes of a good posting and let the matter drop.)* The problems of seniority have been cleared up, too. This apparently is very important, for postings depend to some extent on seniority. I have had to search through the personal files of all the chaplains (and so discovered a lot of interesting things) for all these dates. The personal files show them to be a very mixed bag, I mean the regular ones who have thrived in the sheltered existence now thrown open by war and the arrival of us R.A.F.V.R. types.

The Chaplain-in-Chief, Walkey, is an aging, white-haired Evangelical who is anxious to have lots of chaplains in the service before he retires, for the more he has, the greater his pension will be. Perhaps this is the main reason why I was so welcomed on Bishop George Bell's recommendation *(at my suggestion – the R.N. was my first choice, the R.A.F. the second because I liked the uniform. Bryan could have got me into the army without any delay at all.)* Walkey is a dear old thing who spends his time ignoring routine while Edwards is meticulous about observing it to the point of pedantry. Walkey is clearly a bit bewildered by the sudden expansion of the QJ, Chaplains, department. In September there were about 30 chaplains; by Christmas there were 95; now there are 105 and 110 officiating chaplains.

Walkey has two weaknesses observable to human eyes. His evangelical God knows the others. He loves to hum evangelical hymn tunes which all blend into the current hit, "Run Rabbit Run". He is also an addict to raw Horlicks Malted Milk powder, Bournvita and cocoa, all in powder form, blended with condensed milk. A shelf in the typist's room contains an array of these tins. One afternoon I entered to find the Chief lapping the powders from the various tins out of his hand. The typists were all invited to share in this feast. So was I. I told him that I preferred cocoa mixed with condensed milk, so might I be excused? To which he replied, "I can never get hold of enough condensed milk." The dainties consumed, this relative Air Commodore went back to his office with a circle of milk powder and cocoa round his lips. It has been one of my duties to hint to him that the circle should be removed before he sees visitors. His most regular and least important visitor is an antique major who is attached to the Air Ministry, probably because Walkey likes him. I imagined him to be also a fervent Evangelical but after two minutes conversation he proved himself to be a passionate Roman Catholic with an intense dislike of Queen Elizabeth. He goes into the Chief's room, calls out, "Hello, dear old fellow" and then recites the Angelus aloud. The corridor rings with this devotion. One overhears him shouting to Walkey, "But dear old fellow it's entirely scriptural, I tell you." The RC staff chaplain, Mgr. Beauchamp, doesn't seem to think very highly of him.

The major – I have never found out his name – told me that women should never serve beer and certainly never wine. At periods of menstruation, he explained, they send beer and wine right off. For that reason no women are ever allowed into the champagne cellar at Rheims: "One woman in those cellars, dear old fellow, and the entire stock of wine would be ruined." He thinks little better of Anglican bishops. There isn't one, apparently, with whom he would trust a housemaid after dark. He pleads for a strategic war with Russia and would fight her single-handed on all fronts.

We have had intense cold and snow for a month. It is supposed to have prevented an offensive in France. The politicians are warning us darkly that something very nasty is to be expected in the spring.

Everyone is extremely friendly to R.A.F. chaplains; more so, I am told, than to army ones. This is probably because we look a bit more dashing in our "arse-over-tip" caps. The two chaplains' badges with wings which we wear on our lapels are misinterpreted often as being the brevet which pilots wear or as some decoration for aerial valour. I get embarrassed when people on a bus thank me for "the splendid show you fellows are putting up". I've spent three nights on an RAF station which wasn't operational; and my war effort has been entirely administrative and making up for the lack of syntax on the part of my immediate senior.

(Note for future heroes. My first pay came on January 19th 1940. How wise and lucky I was to bleed the Guardian *so well when they wanted to be shot of me. I was given notice by the* Guardian, *for Owen Hugh Smith had decided to cut down staff on the outbreak of war. The publisher, a brash fellow called Wood, had offered to go to Lambeth and ask the Archbishop to give me a living. I declined his offer, for I knew Lang, the Archbishop, and I could imagine no one better able than Wood to prejudice him against me. I told the proprietor who wanted to give me a month's notice and pay that I*

had the status of an assistant curate and should receive three months'
notice or pay in lieu. He is a very wealthy man, does not know any
church law, and so didn't bother to argue the point, but wrote out a
cheque for £60 or more.)

2nd February 1940

I have arrived at my station and thanks to being at QJ, Chaplains HQ
was able to ensure that it is an operational fighter one – R.A.F. Duxford.
A small Humber van driven by a WAAF met me at Whittlesford station.
The snow is deep and hard, and we had a slippery journey up the
little hill and so to the Mess. My arrival had been signalled this time.

(I reported to the adjutant, Smalley, a retired Indian Army officer.
He was mentally looking back to his life in the Indian army and was
for ever baffled by what to him seemed to be the chaotically free and
easy conditions of life in the Mess. He never showed an emotion. In
the face of the most appalling problem, the most he would say would
be, "Very well then; we'd better get on with it." He spoke usually in
a flat, dry voice, and when, on two occasions only, he spoke with a
little animation, I knew that he was near bursting point. At the height
of our casualties, when one evening we were both alone in the Mess,
I said that the Mess was like the waiting room of a railway station
for pilots, and replacements for lost ones, disappeared and arrived
rapidly. "Not a railway station," he replied, "This is the ante room to
a bloody crematorium." On our first meeting, he gave me a narrow
look and wheeled me into the CO's office.)

There was a warm welcome, for my arrival implied that the station
had suddenly become more important. The Wing Commander, "Pingo"
Lester, is frightened of chaplains, but he seemed pleased enough to
see me. He is obviously terrified that I shall get him into a corner
and ask him some question that he dare not put to himself. *(For this*
last reason he explained that my quarters would be in the village of
Duxford, with transport to convey me to and from the station. This
arrangement was altered after a night or two when he discovered
that I was not going to ask him questions, if only because I suspected

what his answers would be. I knew that they would be beyond my experience for dealing with.)

I was taken across the road to the Mess. The doctor, Browne, also R.A.F.V.R., in the ante room, gave me a very cold and clinical look and exclaimed, "My God! What next? A bloody parson!" But when he saw me drink gin, he unbent. *(We became very close friends. Together we designed a new type of mortuary for the R.A.F.; this grew out of our common experience. Often enough he sent an airman or officer to me with the comment "What's wrong with him is more in your line of country than mine." But he did not understand what I was about. The Christian religion was a mystery to him, and one he was not ready to discuss, though he would always come to my defence in an argument.)*

The entry into the anteroom of the Mess was an ordeal. As a "relative" squadron leader I am one of two senior officers; only the CO has a higher rank. *(This altered soon for the CO became a Group Captain and lots of other people went up by a half ring and became squadron leaders).* So when I went in, hoping not to be noticed, everyone sprang to their feet – "everyone" being without exception fighter pilots – and said, "Good evening, sir". After that no one knew what to do or say next. But the situation was saved by a short pilot officer, with a rather cynical smile, who came across the room and said with a Yorkshire accent, "May I have the honour of getting you a drink, sir?" He expected me, as he told me later, to say "Lime juice". And he was visibly shaken when I asked for gin. *(A day or two later I found out who he was – Peter Watson, one of the enfants terribles of 19 Squadron.)*

That evening passed well enough. I asked questions; everyone liked talking shop. I learned a lot about the station, the three squadrons on it, their history and their present frustrations. I had made up my mind what I would do on the station first of all. So I put the plan into action.

(I spent a lot of time getting to know the pilots for I assumed that when the war really began, they might need help most and would have least time to receive it. I made them talk "shop", which was easy for them, and so I learned as much as I could absorb about Spitfires, Hurricanes and Blenheims, and what they did. We were snow-bound for my first few days. This was a great help to me for the pilots were

Guy's friend Pilot Officer Peter Watson and his pet labrador, Prince.

free to talk. Time and time again, my mind went back to that horrid encounter Bob Emmett and I shared in at Waterloo just after the outbreak of war. As we were leaving the platform, we saw a calf tied by the legs about to be loaded onto a train. Bob asked the porter where the calf was going to. The reply came, "The bloody slaughter, same as you'll be before long."

I was sorry that Bob and I had not parted more easily. Just before I joined the R.A.F., he had been called to his regiment. We had time for another game of squash. It wasn't all that enjoyable because both of us knew that we could not make any date at all for the next game. It became the last in the long series, but as both of us were English to the core, we didn't do the sensible thing which would have been to have accepted the fact and played hell for leather. It was a sad, sad game, not worthy of all the others. And when a day later he called to say goodbye, we were both a bit scratchy and gruff. I still wish that we could have handled it better even though we couldn't see very far ahead, except that we knew that even a short time ahead was further than we liked to think.

I spent a lot of time going round the hangars and asking the fitters and riggers what they were doing and so forth. There were three proud squadrons – 19 Squadron, the most famous of them all, and 66 Squadron with Spitfires and 222 Squadron with Blenheims. There were always enough men from those off-duty or not standing by to "make a service". But I didn't worry very much about this, for I felt that what time I had at Duxford during the long winter was a breathing space to gain experience, knowledge and friends, and most of all to break down my own shyness and reserves for what might lie ahead.

During the first week I turned to Peter Watson for advice and information about the strange world I had entered. He liked giving this advice with a cynical twist. We had not talked very long together before we found out that we were each privately consumed with pride that we were Yorkshire men. He had a way of answering questions with great bluntness and asking blunt ones as well, and expecting blunt answers. Any answer thought to be indirect was labelled as flannel or bullshit. He had entered the service with a short service commission from Harrogate Grammar School. One half of him was in revolt at *the formalities of our life; the other half was consumed with pride in the service. Usually he contrived to be balanced. He was short – the fighter pilots almost of necessity had to be short – quick in reaction and manner; violent in expression and full of thrust. As if to emphasise his shortness, he kept a huge Labrador called Prince. However, this animal was banished to Harrogate when one day it slipped its leash, dashed onto a parade and placed its forepaws round the neck of Leigh Mallory, the AOC of the Group. I was to be accustomed later to the experience of getting to know pilots and being known by them to a degree that in other times and circumstances would have taken many months. In 1940 it took only days where there was rapport.*

Quite soon I confided to Peter that the colour-hoisting parades were dreaded occasions because I was frightened lest I should stammer. At this stage my stammer was a piece of luggage, as it seemed, which I carried about with me, though it was hardly ever used. I suppose I looked for sympathy from Peter. Instead, I got a good kick: "You walk on; you throw up a salute in return for the one that the bog rat (an R.A.F. recruit) gives you. You look round at the shower with contempt; then you start; so shut up."

The conversation took place in my room in a house on the station which had been a married quarter in peace time. I used the drawing room as a bed-sitting room. Peter and some other pilots had the other rooms in the house. I learned that beer was not allowed in one's room, but that beer in one's room was a necessity. This conversation had been conducted with the aid of bottles of Tolly, and, emboldened by another bottle, Peter added, "When you stammer, it's only because you are thinking of yourself and frightened you will stammer." After many more beers, I quickly learned to keep supplies in my room for consumption during the early hours – he said, "For God's sake, stop thinking about yourself and be someone." I was 34 and he must have been about 20. Perhaps he thought he had been too blunt, for he quickly asked me if I would like to fly soon.

In the evenings I would be in my office, doing letters and so on, but really waiting for visitors. And they came. The airmen and the NCO's came apologetically with all sorts of problems, and usually with the humiliating excuse: "I come from 19 Squadron, but my mate in 222 said you had been round their hangar today, so I thought that perhaps ..." There were signal units, some of them very isolated, the kitchens, the police, the antiaircraft units, all to be visited in this seemingly casual way: "Please talk shop."

The evenings ended with a long session in either the officers' or the sergeants' messes with one or two or a group of people talking and asking questions. I went to bed every night, whacked. So I took up again what I had neglected for much too long a time – reading the Bible. I followed the cursus of the lectionary; for some reason I couldn't bring myself, or rather beat down my pride, to recite the office formally. And I tried to make sense of all the facts and information I had gleaned during the day.

The first Sunday wasn't exactly a day of religious revival. There had been no services at all since war broke out. Men who wanted to worship had gone either to Whittlesford or Duxford churches. Next to 19 Squadron hangar was a building marked on the plan as the station church. I reopened it as a temporary measure. It was on the wrong side of the station for quiet; one aircraft taking off and everything in church was heard by God only. I celebrated communion there for a few people on the first Sunday; the next Sunday there were a good many more; during the week when I said mass on two days at least, there was always one other person, usually more than one. I avoided or evaded parade services. This wasn't difficult for we lived in a sense of near crisis; at any moment the whole Luftwaffe, it was thought, would appear overhead.

In the course of the next month I arranged for regular Sunday services at the two AA posts, and later at our two satellite aerodromes, one of them 20 miles away. But there was too much panic, though without cause, for parade services on Sunday, the R.A.F. ritual of colour-hoisting – a cherished relic of our naval origins – survived. I hated this ceremony. Early in the morning men from the squadrons who were going on watch or to the hangars were paraded on the square on the domestic side of the station. The station warrant officer, the officer of the day – usually a pilot who had no love for bullshit either, the adjutant, and on a great occasion the CO, did their bits. In the meantime I was waiting on the touchline since chaplains did not parade. At a given moment I marched onto the *square, took my place in the centre and read prayers, which I had made up for the occasion and kept them revised and polished. Salutes were then thrown up right and left. A fruity voice always said, "Thank you, padre", and I replied in a similar tone, "Thank you, sir" – even if he was the latest bog rat of the service – and went off. This ordeal took place daily, but during the worst of the Battle of Britain it was cancelled, for one day a German aircraft appeared right overhead while I was praying; our AA shells went right over our heads, and I suggested to the CO, who was then Woody Woodhall, that at prayer we offered a splendid target.)*

11ᵗʰ February 1940

First flight: to Horsham St Faith. Pilot Officer Watson. In a Maggy: back via Ely. 19 Squadron. Time in air 60 minutes. Peter flew me in a "Maggy", a Miles Magister, of 19 Squadron, to Horsham St Faith near Norwich, one of our forward stations. We lunched there with the forward flight, and came back over Ely and Cambridge. I thought he was a split-arse pilot for the first flight. There was worse to come later, though. We flew at hedge level most of the way to Horsham St Faith; and on the way back in the cold winter evening, with the fens beneath, he did unspeakable things with the Maggy in the hope of making me sick.

23ʳᵈ February 1940

I took the funeral of P/O Delamere of 222 Squadron and buried his poor bits and pieces at Whittlesford. He was a shy, elegant young man with whom no one could get on terms. He was night-flying for training and he crashed for no apparent reason. There were relatives to be written to. In the evening there was a rowdy dance in the Sergeants Mess. I didn't dance, but talked to anyone who wanted to and propped up the bar.

(Lots came, for beer heightens the theological instincts of the English. I had not felt like going to the dance. I had been shaken a bit by the

crash, by writing to the next of kin, and by the funeral. When I got to my quarters I wondered whether this was how an R.A.F. chaplain should work. I didn't know but it seemed to be the alternative to shutting oneself away both from the spilled blood and guts and from the human beings.

I went on trying to follow that way. The chaplain was the one person who must not be shaken. He must not drown his sorrows. He should not be heavy, whatever his feelings were. He should be there. The policy seemed to work well, for almost always after a dance or a party, I would get people coming to see me to be taught, or to ask for help.)

24*th* February 1940

The net result was that today the very elegant Flight Lieutenant Drew of 222 Squadron took me up in his Blenheim over Cambridge and Thaxted, but we were recalled by a false panic after half an hour. I spent some of the afternoon visiting the detention cells and watching a rugger match. In the evening I organised a new church in what had been the band hut, and then stayed on the flare path till very late watching the Blenheims doing night flying and talking to the flare path crew and the crew of the Chance light. *(I heard by a side wind that the appearance of the chaplain on the flare path to watch night flying was appreciated.)*

25*th* February 1940

Communion in the now converted band hut at 7 a.m. Walked in the snow to Duxford B (AA site) for parade service in the Nissen hut at 9.30 a.m., followed by another parade service at Duxford A at 10.15 a.m. when Flight Lieutenant Faber, the young CO, was present. Brigade Major there in the afternoon corrected notes, sent from the Air Ministry, for commissioned chaplains; evensong at 6.30 p.m. in the band hut with a larger congregation. Squash with Pilot Officer Peter King afterwards and talk till small hours.

(I had found out that the R.A.F. is really a squash playing organisation with flying as a pastime. I played nearly every day, and I did so for

either of two motives. One was enjoyment, for even in 1940 squash had become a major source of pleasure and almost a fount of poetic experience. And of course it was a relief. Nothing of the war or even of the service could be seen or heard on the court. I forgot that my opponents were pilots. The games were moments of release. The other motive was to use squash as an occasion to try to know someone better and to get on easier terms with them. This too paid dividends.)

26th February 1940

Letters. Visited 19 Squadron hangar. Organised bedding for my new quarters which consist of the drawing room of what in peace time would have been the CO's house. Remainder of the rooms are occupied by pilots of 19 Squadron.

Peter Watson took me for a flight in a Maggie in the afternoon. We went to Cambridge and then flew along the river towards Ely, coming down (if that was possible – Peter flew at hedge height most of the afternoon: he was working something off) to look at the University Eight at Baits Bite. Then continued with low flying and hedge-hopping to Ely. Once round the cathedral, then to the R.A.F. hospital, and returned via the sugar beet factory where the aircraft was conveniently tipped so that I could look down a factory chimney. Visibility was under a mile at 1000 feet and worse at 2000. Found I couldn't relax very well and let myself drop and turn with the aircraft. Possible reason was that Peter was being deliberately split-arse in his flying. We were up 45 minutes.

The RC chaplain called this afternoon at 5 p.m. Ramsden called at 5.30 p.m. and talked till I had a confirmation class at 6.30 p.m. Went to a flick in the NAAFI in the evening.

27th February 1940

Letters and calls on the station all the morning. Afternoon talking to airmen in the NAAFI. Squash with Peter King after tea. 5.30 – 7.30

p.m.: long talks with airmen in my room before dinner. Evening in the WAAF Officers Mess.

28th February 1940

Punchard (local vicar) here this morning. Walked in the afternoon round the aerodrome talking to the guards. Told them about new leave arrangements and stayed for an hour or more. Examined a Wellington bomber on my way back: the first one I've seen close at hand. Squash with Peter. NAAFI concert. Peter Watson came and talked afterwards. Have been told by the CO that I must do my best to get the pilots to go to bed early and to take more exercise.

29th February 1940

Tried to write an address this morning without success; further attempt this afternoon. Searched SHQ files for a letter on welfare. Confirmation class at 6 p.m. "Surgery hours" longer than usual and particularly full about questions re marriage. One airman asked my advice on first night behaviour; the first night is to be spent in the Charing Cross Hotel. Did he undress in the same room as his wife? A sergeant who is RC wants to be received into the C of E.

19 Squadron were night flying after dinner. Went out to the Chance light to watch. Bitterly cold and the wind cut through my great coat. Clouston and Baker with me. We didn't have to run it for once. Trenchard crashed while we were there. He had been missed, and we were looking for his lights when the Ops room phoned that he had crashed three miles from Whittlesford. Heard later that he was killed at once. Clouston, who is a flight commander, went off at once to the pilots' room. I stayed with Baker, and when the last aircraft was down, we walked back across the aerodrome to the Mess feeling very heavy. I stayed in the Mess, trying to make conversation and keep people from brooding over Trenchard.

(There were a crowd of pilots in the anteroom, sitting about silently and pretending to read "Flight" or the "Aeroplane". I forced

conversation and after a while there was a roaring discussion about the moral and personal habits of air officers and group captains which lasted till the small hours.)

Midnight – 2 a.m. – Talked to Watson who came off-duty as Orderly Officer.

(I was just about to get into bed feeling that I had done my stint when Peter appeared with beer and questions following upon Trenchard's death. It was a relief to be able to talk realistically to him, not about Trenchard, but about the things which we keep concealed for the most part beneath the surface. What happens when you die? Is it wrong to be frightened of dying? How should you live if you are twenty and will be dead by the end of the summer? This was the first of many talks which only appeared sad and startling in retrospect. At the time they seemed almost to be part of service shop. Most of the pilots who came late at night to drink beer and talk followed this one topic, and when we became really involved in the war in May, they talked almost every night. But Peter and, later on, Harold Oxlin, pushed the subject to the frontiers and we talked without restraint. With the others, I had always to be considering what to say, how best to say it, not only in principle, but to the person. With these two, the talk was unselfconscious.)

1ˢᵗ March 1940

At last the talk for Sunday has got into better shape though not what I like. There it must stay. Flew to Horsham St Faith with Peter at midday. Lovely day; no clouds till we got to Norwich; icy wind. I've never flown in such fine weather; we could see the coast long before Norwich and the sun shining on the cold, cold sea. There was a strong head wind and we took 50 mins going. Only one burst of low flying over the range near Newmarket. We lunched at Horsham St Faith with "Dimmy", Douglas Bader, "Chiefy" Brinsden, Mathieson and two Sergeant Pilots – beer, steak, fruit salad, all of which we had brought with us. I talked to the airmen and then waited for a flight to return. It had been out investigating an alleged "raid" at 15000 feet above

Dereham. One of our bombers, I expect. Peter got back to Duxford at 4 p.m. taking only 40 minutes. Rather cloudier; we flew at 1500 and sang "The Red Flag" and the "Internationale" to each other over the intercom. A lovely day with the best company, with whom I now feel very much at ease. Stomach much happier with flying and certainly better than last time. God, it's lovely to be up there. Work after tea in the office. Walked with Michael Lyne, Peter and Peter King to the Red Lion and back, mainly for exercise. Lovely sunset over the plateau. Film in the garage hangar.

(The field of acquaintances and friends grew wider and very often deeper. With Peter Watson also came Michael Lyne who was his close friend. They were opposites in many respects. Peter enjoyed the excitement of flying. He was rash by nature and impulsive. He did not read much, though every night he looked at a page of a small dictionary that went everywhere with him in order to widen his vocabulary. Michael was a "regular" and had graduated from Cranwell and so was one of the elite. He was widely-read, carful in expression and with a quick wit. He was not rash by any means, for he believed in a mystique of the air. Deep down, I think, he believed that a pilot is almost a superman. He would not admit this, although he did maintain that a pilot by the experience of his flying became someone different and special. Flying to him was an aesthetic experience, but it was to others who thought less deeply. He would argue that this experience makes one different; he would not admit superior, except when he was talking about one or other of his friends. They were all mortal men, but the pilots were less mortal than ordinary humanity. Because a pilot was serious in purpose, Michael would argue that therefore a higher and more exacting standard of moral conduct and mental discipline was demanded of him. We were to meet several times during the war after I had left Duxford, and always wherever we met, whether at Gibraltar or in Cairo, he brought with him this infused sense of difference. When years after the war, I met him near Ninfield and at Rotherfield, and he was grown into an Air Vice Marshal, he still carried unconsciously this nimbus with him. Thelma talked about this with Joy, his wife, who said that she believed that, in his heart of hearts, Michael considered that pilots were a different caste of men, though he was too simple and humble to apply that to himself.

I saw him last in 1962. He had not changed a lot. There was the same vivacity, the same assuredness – not quite the same as self-assurance – and the same probing questions and mordant humour. Until the end of the Battle of Britain he was a constant companion in the Mess and outside, off-duty. By off-duty, I mean the companion on innumerable visits to pubs nearby, to pubs in Cambridge and to visits to our flat in Cambridge and to our cottage at Linton.)

Long talk in the anteroom with Smalley and Nicholls, the adjutant of 19 Squadron and a veteran of the first war. *(Nicholls had been a pilot in the first war and could never forget it. Between him and the pilots grew up a love-hate relationship. They liked him for the way he fought for their needs and stood up for them. They disliked him for the many sentences which began "When I flew with Sopwiths, we..." etc. He drank too much. He was good to me, and trusted me.)*

Bed in the small hours.

2nd *March 1940*

Paid various calls on the station. Walked to Whittlesford to see the vicar about some banns and Trenchard's funeral. Walked from there to Duxford to negotiate about a standard wreath and a standard charge for it in case we have many more funerals. Returned across the aerodrome. Even better day than yesterday, with less wind and no cloud.

Went up at 3 p.m. with P/O Broadbent of 222 Squadron in a Blenheim on an interception. Wore a "Mae West" for the first time. We flew to Norwich and circled there for half an hour at 6000 feet. We then got a line and went out to sea at 13000 feet over Cromer.

We saw the incoming German plane but failed either to intercept or to identify it. There was another interception near us which was more successful. This was ten miles out to sea off Sheringham. The enemy had shot up a lightship this morning. Hence our call. This was the most enjoyable flight I've had: the weather was wonderful. You could see halfway up the Lincs coast and down to Felixstowe. I know the ground plan of Norwich pretty well having looked at it for

Bristol Blenheims of No. 222 Squadron, January 1940. Guy flew with Duxford pilots on many occasions – usually leisurely cross-country flights in the station's Miles Magister, but sometimes in a Blenheim. HU 58248

an hour. We flew back in tight formation with another Blenheim, and as a result our Klaxon horn was going most of the time, for the other Blenheim wasn't in a hurry, and we kept getting near stalling speed as we were following it. Maximum speed during the flight was 250 mph. There was some sensation of speed but only by comparison with the Maggy. The sea looked good – blue and not grey as the North Sea usually looks. Saw some minesweepers a long way out. Morant who was the other interceptor went out 70 miles over the sea.

Got back at 5.10 p.m.

Worked in the office after tea and had a man to see me. Went out on the flare path this evening to the Chance light. Its engine failed just as a Blenheim wanted to land. But he was given the green light and all was well. The best night flying we've had. All the stars and all the searchlights on show. Formation flying is good if deafening.

3rd March 1940

The finest day of the year and warm – warm enough to sit out. Communion in the band hut at 7 a.m. Walked with Prince (Peter's dog) to Thriplow for services on the AA sites and Prince came back in Transport. Service at Whittlesford AA site. Shooting with revolvers at the fire alarm bell after lunch. No one was hurt. The bell was hit once. Oh yes, Curtis was hit, but it didn't hurt, tough guy! Looked up answers to problems in Kings Regulations after lunch; letters. Evensong.

With Kester (liaison officer with the R.A.F. for searchlights and AA) went to the Ops room and then to the flare path. We had an exciting run to the Chance light; just as we were half way across the path, the light went on and we saw a Spitfire coming down on us. It was a damn hard run. No accidents this evening but some near misses. It is a crowning folly of civilisation that men should practise night flying at 250 mph or more in darkness, though after Trenchard's death we have had some more lights.

(Many of us were oppressed by the lack of imagination which had led to his death and that of several others through night flying training. The flare path and the other lights were reduced to the operational minimum as though always there was a raid overhead or immediately expected. As a result of Trenchard's death, there was a protest made and, until the war became lively and there was no more night flying training, more lights were allowed.)

The talk in the Mess this evening was about bailing out. It seems that, even if your parachute doesn't open, you remain conscious till you make your hole in the ground. The station engineering officer told us of finger nails torn away in attempts to open the parachute somehow when the release device has failed or the wearer has lost his head and can't find the press release.

4th March 1940

Long talk with Drew, a pilot of 222 Squadron, this morning at Mermagen, the Squadron CO's, request. There are doubts about his morale. *(I was asked to discover whether his morale was going and if so what the causes were. I had few standards on which to work. I could only go by what I had seen and heard during the short while I had been on the station, and I knew I ought to allow for the difference in temperament between the fighter pilots and those of 222 Squadron who were using light bomber aircraft as fighters. Rightly, they were slower and more phlegmatic in temperament.)*

Talked to WAAFs and airmen on the station this afternoon.

Trenchard's funeral. A fine day and a warm one for it. It was a particularly unhappy affair. His fiancée was there: her looks were sufficient to make one want to cry. I tried to say good things to her when the service was over. The waste, the criminal waste that these funerals represent. Poor 19 Squadron has been in the depths all day. Clouston, who was in charge of the funeral party, was uneasy, and with reason, for he gets married tomorrow. The situation was all the more cruel because I had spent most of the morning talking to Drew. I thought at the end of our talk that this pilot's morale was not cracking; what he had was good, but inadequate for his flying duties. So a party with champagne taken down to the Red Lion was held. Party ended at about 2 a.m. in the kitchen of the Mess, with myself and Pilot Officer Nigel Browne as the survivors eating dripping toast. Nigel flies helicopters and everything is so secret that we all know what it's about but daren't show it.

(*This was the first time that Nigel and I had got on terms. He was flying a helicopter on secret duties at Duxford; either we were intrigued to know what the duties were or else pilots were jealous that a young man of their age should apparently be living a death-free life in the air, or else, and this applied to the older men, they were contemptuous of his apparent duties. As the year wore on we became great friends, if never very intimate; he was one of Robert's godfathers, because Thelma and I liked him so much and he was solid.*)

Sometime during the evening John Petre, a pilot of 19 Squadron, and I had had a long ontological discussion, caused by Trenchard's death. The aftermath of Trenchard's funeral was to induce John Petre to come and talk about death. But to pluck up the courage to do this (*John was brave anyway*), John had been up to Clouston's wedding party for drinks (*Clouston being a long way away by that time*).

5ᵗʰ March 1940

Peter Wansey, now chaplain to searchlights, called and I took him round the aerodrome. Letters. Played squash with Bob Oxspring from

Sheffield. Office, dinner, confirmation class.

6th March 1940

Went on 48 hours leave. Peter flew me to Weybridge. Time 40 minutes. We went via Welwyn, Hatfield, Denham, and Slough and then picked our way avoiding balloons across Runnymede to Weybridge. Great sensation when we landed as Weybridge is most secret, and landing is forbidden. Peter just touched down and I leaped off. While everyone was looking at the aircraft and wondering what to do, I made for the exit, unobserved, and Peter took off. I caught the 4.16 p.m. to Esher. An exciting way to come home on leave and also a cheap one.

8th March 1940

Got back here with the Hillman at 3.30 p.m. Interviews with airmen from 5.30 p.m. till 10 p.m. with a break for dinner.

9th March 1940

Finished sermon. Went to Cambridge and bought a new squash racquet. Saw Evelyn, Michael and Roger Williams. Played squash with Lacey and was badly beaten. Pub crawl in the Grantchester area with Peter. Bed at 1 a.m.

10th March 1940

Usual services. Went to Cambridge to say goodbye to Michael (*Williams, son of Selwyn don*) who is going to France. Early to bed as dead tired.

11ᵗʰ March 1940

Wrestled with lecture for tomorrow and sermon. Bitted about on camp in the morning and after lunch. More work on lecture. Letters; interviews. Crawled about a Miles Master. Confirmation class. Early to bed with incipient cold.

12ᵗʰ March 1940

Talked to group of clergy and laity (civilian) at St Andrews, Whittlesford about "Eternal Life" which was the title given me but I interpreted it as drawing on what experience I have gained from these few weeks spent in preparing people for eternal life. Then another lecture about Spiritualism (from my work on the Archbishop's commission). Stayed to lunch. Visited 222 Squadron hangar. Spent an hour working in Intelligence. Interviews with airmen. Session in the Ops room. Peter Watson, Peter King and Drew talking here till 11 p.m. Bed.

13ᵗʰ March 1940

Vain attempt to write Sunday's address this morning. Took church funds and Peter to Cambridge (Peter for compulsory hair cut).

"Pingo" Lester, the CO, has gone, to everyone's relief. *(He had never grown out of being a fighter pilot; he was jumpy, nervy and liable to private hysteria. According to Peter, he was liable to other and darker troubles as well.)*

The new station commander is Woodhall. Had tea with him and his monocle. *(We were jerked out of our curious war and our reserved attitude to it by the arrival of the new CO, who was promoted to Group Captain almost on arrival. He proved himself from the first to be the man for us. He drank like a fish and concealed the effects or almost always, but there was nothing dark about him that needed hiding. Soon after his arrival he sent for me and talked about the morale and discipline of the pilots. I was to get them to bed earlier. I was to*

'Woody' Woodhall, Station Commander at Duxford during the Battle of Britain, with whom Guy formed a close working relationship. 'Woody' finished the war as a Group Captain, and one of the most widely-respected fighter controllers in the RAF. CH 1386

see that they drank less. To this one, I asked him, "But how, sir?" "By drinking with them yourself and setting an example."

By good fortune, two events happened which led to mutual trust. Everyone, young and old alike, disliked an officer called Oades. He made himself so unpopular with the pilots that one evening, without my realising what had happened, the tyres of his car were deflated. There was a row; he complained formally to the CO. He wanted a court martial. Woody sent for me. He believed, and rightly, that I knew who was responsible. I described Oades in the Mess; Woody screwed his monocle into his eye and glared at me. All he had to say when I had finished was "What do you propose to do, Padre?"

"To take this sordid little worry off your hands, sir."

So, while Oades was engaged with the CO, his tyres were pumped up again. He returned to lunch in the Mess, content – if not content, at least mollified.

On the second occasion, 15th March, the WMF officers gave a dance to celebrate Woody's arrival at the station. This was a lugubrious affair, and no one enjoyed it except Woody who had brought his squeeze box with him and played it ad nauseam. Peter showed his nausea, having drunk too much. He was got out of the room, but not without some incidents. These were the more tiresome because I was trying to cover them up while talking to the new WAAF CO who believed that the apparition of Ramsay MacDonald was a powerful spiritual healer. Sensing trouble, as soon as I woke up in the morning I roused Peter and made him absorb Eno's. He was very cross and stood on his head on the bed to show how sober he was. I was not convinced. The remainder of 19 Squadron flew on detachment to Digby, leaving Peter behind. Woody sent for me and asked what should be done. With a faint heart, I said, "Leave it to me, sir" and, to my surprise, he agreed. I returned to quarters and tore a strip off Peter.)

Held a bible class, on request, this evening. It lasted nearly two hours. It may be difficult as all the members are fundamentalists. Went back to the Mess and talked with "Ace" Pace about his engagement and, I hope, helped him in a sticky problem. Peter came and talked in my room about many things in general till the small hours.

"Ace" Pace is unique. He is 22 or 23, perhaps not as much. A very good pilot. He is soaked in the traditions of the First World War and the primitive air force. He loves singing the songs that allegedly the R.A.F. used to sing way back but are too macabre to be sung now e.g. "Good luck to the next man who dies" and "A poor wounded airman lay dying". He might have stepped out of a novel. But he is as direct and simple as they are made, and brave.

(He was a graduate of Cranwell and belonging to 19 Squadron. But he had never caught up with this war. He lived in the days of "Dawn Patrol"– the title of a film about the R.A.F. in the First World War. He loved flying Spitfires, not because they were the last thing in fighters but because the heroes of the first war had fought in their versions of the final design of the Spitfire. He alone of everyone in the Mess admired the water cooler in the anteroom of a seaplane which had force landed in the North Sea – the aircraft was on fire. I labelled the picture "Which way will you die in the R.A.F. – by drowning or

*burning?" In the end we got it removed. He was an incredible figure,
for he was a real flash-back; the older men liked him for he doted
on them and lapped up their most bogus stories. He was fighting in
another war. He played the most violent game of squash of anyone I
have ever met. He played to win, regardless of injury to his opponent.)*

Had a talk with Peter about nothing in particular and many things
in general before turning in.

14th March 1940

Woken up at 6 a.m. by Peter using my telephone to find out what
was "the state" of his squadron. I was a bit short with him. This
had "murdered sleep". Two inches of snow and more falling. Long
talk with a Sergeant Pilot of 222 Squadron about "rotol and pitch".
Intelligence work this afternoon. Letters morning and afternoon.
Wasted early afternoon waiting for an airman who didn't come to
see me: my fault for mistaking the afternoon. Snowing off and on all
day. Watched boxing which I have organised this evening. One man
entirely knocked out. The boxing instructor who has been sent here to
make for healthy exercise and sport is an ex-champion. He is seldom
sober; but despite this he seems willing to be cooperative. Nicholls,
who apparently was a boxer in his distant past, returned to my room
afterwards and talked till 1 a.m.

15th March 1940

Have acquired a magnificent pair of wellington boots from
stores. Booked room for Thel at "Le Lion Rouge" (The Red Lion,
Whittlesford). Went into Cambridge with Peter and dined at the Arts
Restaurant (preceded by pints in the Red Cow. The place is changed:
one thought the Red Cow a centre of stability in a changing world).

Went onto the Union where we drank many ports. Peter's capacity
for beer is almost equalled by the way in which he consumes port:
he doesn't drink it – he absorbs it. Swartout was there sitting in the

same chair that he occupied when I was an undergraduate and he was editor of the *Granta*. He listened to our conversation which may have surprised him. Back here to a dance. Talked to the WAAF CO, to Ace Pace's fiancée and to Mrs Dainty who told me of spiritual healing obtained through the apparition of Ramsay MacDonald. Peter was not at his best at the dance; put up some blacks and was finally escorted to bed. Self tired but sober enough.

16th March 1940

Filled Peter up with Eno's first thing. He was indignant at my suggestion that he had drunk too much last night or might be feeling less than acutely fit: to prove this (which it didn't) he stood on his head on getting out of bed. Watched 19 Squadron leave for Digby. Peter left behind, so I ticked him off for last night. Everyone else in the Mess except me rather hang-overy; more lime juice than gin is being consumed today. Confirmation class. Ghastly officers concert this evening. Applee, the second M.O. who is a very self-conscious Jew and rather greasy, did a speciality dance with the WAAF CO. No one knew whether it was serious or satire. I was appealed to for guidance but felt unable to help.

17th March 1940

Communion at 8 a.m. All other services as usual. Supper with the WAAF officers and Nicholls.

18th March 1940

Long interview with Woody, the new CO. He wants me to be responsible for sports and entertainment. Talking about discipline etc. among younger officers, though how I can control a box of fireworks who realise they may be near death I don't know.

I managed to white-wash Peter with the CO. Met Thel at the station and stayed till I took Kearsley and Ramsden, the confirmees, to Pampisford. After the service, returned to the Red Lion. Peter came in for a lift back from the station and owing to "readiness" we came back about 10.30 p.m.

19th March 1940

Went on working parade for prayers (The new CO's innovation. Smalley has said, "The one good thing about new brooms is that when they sweep clean they break their bloody handles.") Only officer there; very difficult as I am not executive. Prayers thrown in my teeth by the wind and the rain. Went to Cambridge with Thel to house-hunt and have struck lucky in Panton Street. Lunch at the KP Restaurant; interviews here this afternoon; dinner with Thel at the Red Lion.

20th March 1940

Breakfast with Thel who went to Cambridge by train. Wrote addresses and looked up men in the morning and afternoon. Bible class (thin ice) in the evening. Séance with Drew and Peter.

21st March 1940

In more civilised times, Maunday Thursday. Morning in sick bay. Applee tells me he writes sonnets and that he will show them to me if I make him drunk enough. We are all alerted and have been since early this morning. Ack Ack are standing by at immediate. Borrowed anthologies from Michael Lyne – early to bed tonight. Many rumours that 19 Squadron may be moved to France. This is a dismal outlook for everyone for, virtually, they are Duxford, and, though 66 Squadron comes a close second in prestige, even 66 are considered to be intruders by 19 Squadron because they didn't get their Spitfires the first of any squadron in the R.A.F.

Mysterious bumps and crashes at the H site this evening. There is the coincidence that two Spits cut out twenty feet up after taking off and sabotage is suspected. Wild party in Cambridge last night at which I was not present; centred round the so-called rugger XV. Curtis fell out of the car at 20 mph on the way back. He is covered with bandages from head to foot and need only go into Cambridge to live on free drinks for ever for he looks like one of the heroes of the Sylt bombing.

22nd March 1940

Took services at AA sites and also in Thriplow church. This was the simplest worship and, I hope, the plainest Christian preaching. This has been the strangest Good Friday since I was in Rome with Edward Ratcliffe. Carter (assistant station adjutant) told me that the following signal bas been received: "God has sent us a child. Will you marry me now?"

(Carter, fat, fair and forty, was the administrative officer with the nickname of 'Ming", who was the giant Panda in the Zoo. He was, as it were, my liaison with the older men, and regularly he put me in touch with some aging officer who was cracking, or whose marriage was going wrong, or who was drinking too much or trying to recapture lost youth. Both he and Nicholls were veterans of the First World War, but, unlike the other "deadbeats" in the Mess, Carter seldom mentioned it, and this was held to his credit.)

After evensong and supper, played billiards with Michael and lost by 5 in a game of 125 up. Not too bad after ten years of no practice. SOS from Cambridge Provost Marshal. Would I go to the Great Northern Hotel and fetch John Baker who was stranded there? It was an opportunity that might later give me a chance with him. He presents problems in all manner of ways. So I went, taking Peter and Prince the dog with me by way of chaperons – you never know what may be in store at the Great Northern Hotel; so I met Wendy, the legend of 19 Squadron. I've never seen a girl with less expression on her face though no doubt she is well-equipped otherwise. Her mother is obviously anxious that an R.A.F. officer should be captured for her. Back here at 11.30 p.m. John put to bed, and Peter and I talked. A strange Good Friday but what a nice one.

23rd March 1940

Got ready for tomorrow and generally made myself useful. New WAAF CO has arrived, thank God. But first impressions suggest that she is a shocker. She is a parson's wife and wants to run the WAAFs like a Sunday school. Wants me to hold compulsory parade services for them. She seems to be a maniac for compulsory everything (no wonder her husband said, "Join up, my dear, your duty is clear.") We all agreed that she must be told how we do things here. Carter has told her that I know best and that she mustn't stick her nose in. Party in the WAAF Mess to meet her. CO there, plus his sister, Mermagen, the squadron leader of 222 Squadron, Browne, the doctor and Carter and me. Browne, early on, got called away by the obvious subterfuge of a phone message from the sick bay. Wonder what the WAAF CO thought about it all, particularly when the station commander, without much invitation, recited, "Life begins at 40". She is a grim piece, but she confided in me that, now she is away from a parish, she feels free to be natural for the first time in years. Poor dear. Don't I know that feeling?

Easter Day 1940

Celebrations and parade services at the AA posts. Lovely fine day and sat out in the garden this afternoon. Good congregation at evensong, and I found out by chance that some of the people had come back from Cambridge to be present. That encourages me. Long talk with Heath (whose morale is unjustly doubted).

Easter Monday 1940

To Cambridge to talk to Miss Ferguson, Thel's landlady. Saw Evelyn Williams and talked about Michael who is, of her two sons, the apple of her eye. Squash with Brinsden in which I was beaten 8–1. He has red hair and is a ball of fire, off and on the court. He is by far the best player on the station. Early to bed but preceded by an orgy of ginger beer with Peter: six bottles and a bar of chocolate.

26ᵗʰ March 1940

Met John Widdows *(later Chichester diocesan registrar)* at Royston for lunch. We came back here and talked about aircraft till 4 p.m. when I drove him back to Royston. It was raining hard so he had to be content with a distant view of the Spits from the road. We are all grounded. Went to the station cinema out of duty and saw "Windbag the Sailor" with Will Hay. Not his best. Meant to go early to bed but Peter and Ace Pace came and talked till 1 a.m.

27ᵗʰ March 1940

Flew with Peter in the Maggy to Horsham St Faith to call on the vicar who is officiating chaplain. Peter asked me if I would loop. Was yellow and shouted "No" over the intercom and added various names. He acquiesced but made me suffer in other ways; some low flying which no longer makes me feel frightened; some low turns which I don't enjoy but feel should endure, and a roll. We flew low all the way and very, very low for the greater part of it. I am beginning to know the heaths outside Thetford very well. The stomach is now conquered. It was an extremely windy and bumpy day. Flew back with Mathieson and sat in the front seat. The return was even bumpier with one colossal air-pocket near Thetford. We had the wind behind us and, though the Maggy was tossed about like a leaf, got back fast enough and made an appalling landing in three huge bounces. It was an exciting flight as the switches were not working well and there was more than the usual chance that the engine might have cut. Round the camp this afternoon. Presided over sports officers meeting. Squash with Michael Lyne. Growing discussion class this evening which lasted from 8.15 p.m. to 10.45 p.m.

29th March 1940

Went to Cambridge this afternoon to look for a camera and found one at the pawnbrokers in Bridge Street. Met Heath's fiancée. Sergeant's dance this evening but stayed only a short time as I am bunged up with a cold. Another pilot in the 222 Squadron has been killed. He had been away on a course and returned two days ago. He looped a Maggy at 500 feet and went straight in at Fowlmere. Dimmy and Curtis who were also up in a Maggy saw it. Dimmy has been placed under close arrest because it is suggested, I think wrongly, that they were playing a game of follow my leader in which Dimmy was the leader. Poor Doc' Browne, the MO, is also involved. His fiancée is staying near here. He took a chance and went to Shelford to see her and their new house. The crash happened while he was off the station. He is up for a court of inquiry.

1st April 1940

Pilot Officer Griffiths' funeral at Whittlesford this afternoon. Tea with Punchard afterwards. He talked interestingly about his work as chaplain to a mental hospital. There has been a change round of pilots' quarters so that they will be easier to call for readiness. Peter has now left the "Vicarage". The house is quieter, if duller, and it's not so easy to consult unobtrusively that source of blunt Yorkshire wisdom and common sense on R.A.F. matters. Who comes to replace Peter and Drew is not yet settled, though I think that Squadron Leader Welch's things have been moved in.

After dinner I went with Peter and Michael Lyne to the pub at Trumpington where Thel, Michael Williams and had cider last year when war seemed too crazy a prospect to be possible. Then we went to the Green Man at Grantchester, for explained to them that it was there really that passed the Law Tripos and much else. Coming back, we left the car, and walked to Byron's Pool, there to pay tribute to his shade in customary form.

2nd April 1940

Chased round the camp this morning organising games. Had lunch with Peter Wansey at the Militia Camp at Royston but left when he started to talk about the Oxford Group and tried to rope me in.

Curtis has asked me to restore my wellington boots to store. I explained my embarrassment. I may not keep drink in my quarters I have no cupboards; so I can only keep it concealed in my boots. I said I would return the boots when the port was finished.

John Baker behaved badly in the Mess last night and this morning. He drank too much last night. I was told to "brown him off" for unseemly behaviour. I asked Peter the gentlest way to do it. He told me to follow peace time R.A.F. rules which John would understand and to send for him officially. So I did. This evening John turned up in hat and gloves (quite rightly). Walked smartly into my room, saluted, and said, "You sent for me, sir." So I said, "Yes, Baker" for I was surprised at the R.A.F. tradition coming to life. I told him what I thought of him, not violently or roughly but in his own language, for like him, and asked for any comments (again in the tradition). He replied, "I never expected to hear such words coming from a service chaplain". To which I replied, "I thought I ought to use words which you would understand. That will be all". So he saluted smartly and went out. I then went over to the Mess and bought him a drink. I feel this was all in the best tight-lipped traditions of the R.A.F.

I went to bed early.

3ʳᵈ April 1940

Told I had done just right with John. More organising sports and bitting about adjutants' offices. This afternoon at the carefully organised run 4 turned up: God save all the others. Had a long interview with Nicholls and Flight Sergeant Berry about a W.E.M. (Wireless and Electrical Mechanic) who has been behaving improperly with a Flight Sergeant in 19 Squadron. The Flight Sergeant was posted within an hour. Nicholls has taken up his residence in my house and in Peter's room, so the continuity with 19 Squadron is preserved.

German aircraft over here this afternoon at 10,000 feet. Bags of headiness and panic. Cloud was so thick that we couldn't see him or he us. Mermagen went up but couldn't find him. His plot was an unbroken one from the "line of action" over to Duxford and then to London.

Woody called a formal Mess meeting in the anteroom this evening. This is all in R.A.F. peace time tradition, but he points out that we aren't fighting a proper war yet (though there are signs that things are not going to be pleasant for much longer). He thinks a touch of formality will help to keep discipline, not least among the pilots who, because they aren't being killed, haven't enough to do.

Today is also Peter's birthday. He announced that he wouldn't come to the Mess meeting but would have a party (of one if necessary) instead. Pointed out to him that he could have the party after the Mess meeting; that if he cut the meeting, there would be trouble with Woody who remembers his behaviour at the WAAF party. We suggested that he should begin his party at the Red Lion before the meeting, come to the meeting and then go on with the party. Nicky (Nicholls) and self had a terrific struggle with him. We were told we were bullshitting; that he was surprised we should be bullshitters. I told him I would do my best to have him put under arrest, since I can't put anyone under arrest myself; Nicky agreed, and so Peter came, black as thunder. I was appointed messing officer.

When the meeting was over and Woody was still in the anteroom having gins with us, and we were all having a rather peace time R.A.F. conversation (as I imagine) with lots of "Sirs" and so on, I noticed through the portholes of the wing doors to the anteroom that there was some scuffling going on in the corridor; there was also a good deal of noise. I made an excuse to leave the group and went to see if all was as I feared. It was. Peter was drinking Pimms No 1 by the pint and had got well-oiled. So I put on my most frigid manner and told him to go away. I could foresee that, if the scuffling and noise went on, the worst "black" of all would be put up and he would probably say something funny but insubordinate about the Group Captain, in the strongest Yorkshire accent. He went away with John Baker and others, and trouble was averted. I went back into the anteroom and resumed the "Sir" conversation.

4th April 1940

A day of snuffles and snorts from a stifling catarrh which seemed to be made worse by playing squash with Bob Oxspring.

5th April 1940

Nostalgia for Yorkshire. Peter described to me how good York station would look when he arrived there this evening on his seven days leave. "You've got her! You've got her! God's got her!" Bang!

6th April 1940

Flight for me to Driffield in a Maggy with Bob Oxspring on Monday is washed out as he is posted on a parachute course. Helped Kester and Ball to check the bar stock, a pleasant if self-appointed and not really necessary duty. Afterwards went with Kester to the Red Lion where Woody and his sister were. After that we went to Highfield, his house off the station; waited for him outside with a bottle of whiskey; but getting impatient we went in by the back door and drank whiskey till he came.

Stayed till midnight. I think this has done good, for I sense that

Woody may want some help later on and I'm anxious that he should be on easy terms with me.

7th April 1940

Not very fresh and catarrh not improved by last night. Last hope of flying to Driffield (with Franky Brinsden) washed out as Maggy u/s. So I went by road, arriving at Bridlington at 4.30 p.m. The Great North Road and the rest of the way seemed to be lined with R.A.F. stations on which Hampdens and Wellingtons were bombing up. Found father and mother well enough but very quiet. Father goes to Hull every day; mother has to walk for the shopping as the cars are laid up – no one to drive.

9th April 1940

Germany invades Norway and Denmark. So it has started. This short time at Bridlington has made me feel afresh the horror and futility of the war. I know I am sentimental about Yorkshire. The clouds were high as I came back over the Wolds yesterday and spring was in the weather, and there should have been lots of hope in one's heart. It looked like the best country in all the whole world. The Wold road, either via Market Weighton or via York, always grips me. It seems so wicked that the Yorkshire pilots at Duxford, for example, Peter, Peter King, John Baker and Bob Oxpring, may not see Flamborough Head again where I drove mother this time, or drive up Garrowby Hill again to Bridlington. When I was their age, I felt morally certain I had years left in which to go over the Moors and Dales. If you want to know what a Yorkshire man thinks about the Dales, ask Peter. His reply would have warmed Basil Woodd's heart (*my first vicar*).

But by June who will be left? Please God all of them but almost certainly not. And we shall be weeping for our children "because they are not". Unlike real children, these young men are mature enough to know what they miss, as it seems to them, if they go down. Of course as a Christian, I should say "This doesn't matter; the real life starts when this one ends". I know that is true and I believe it but if the physical joys are pagan, then one is still fond of them. How dreadful to die before finding out how much better life is at 30 than it was even at 22, or how happy marriage can be.

Mother has been machine gunned while coming home from shopping at Bridlington and had to lie down in the gutter. Father's train to Hull is machine gunned now and then by raiders. But both of them spoke about these things without surprise or resentment. Victorians are tough. Saw a Hampden chasing a German raider over Bridlington Bay last night. German got away.

10th April 1940

I got back to Duxford at 3.30 p.m. and found packets of work and papers awaiting me. Feeling less browned off.

11th April 1940

Bible class in the evening. How it staggers on, I don't know, but I manage to preside without disturbing the fundamentalists. Then to the Corporals Dance where I was compelled to dance otherwise feelings would have been hurt. The dances were mainly cutting in. This was tantalising as one danced only short dances with the prettier WAAFs. Lost my heart to one who was particularly minx-ish.

12th April 1940

Went with Peter and John Baker to Cambridge for a haircut. Afterwards to a flick, and then after a visit to the Baron of Beef and the Red Lion, back here for Guest Night. John Baker has the idea that one only goes into a pub in order to drink too much. Browned him off for that; he also received a more paternal address from Peter (pot calling kettle black).

The Guest Night was really to say goodbye to Pingo Lester (the old CO) and Dransfield (the MO who left before I came). It was successful. Woody played his accordion without waiting to be asked, and sang, monocle in eye; his eyes blood-shot and looking like two poached eggs on stalks. Everyone sang till 12.15 a.m. when all went quietly to bed leaving Dransfield drunk and asleep on a sofa in the anteroom.

There was a fuss with John Baker. We had a formal Mess dinner; grace, the loyal toast etc. in the tradition. John Baker was going to cut it for a party. For once benevolent angels and I intervened to save him from his folly and rough words had not to be used.

13th April 1940

Long, fatherly and wise talk from Peter for most of the morning, mostly concerned with what I could do for John Baker (the assumption in Peter's mind being, I think, that John will survive him). Long talk with Woody and Kester in Woody's house after tea. Am getting on really close terms with Woody for I don't think he has hitherto been on very close terms with any chaplain. After dinner produced the port from my wellington boot and shared it with Nicky and Peter, but put it away just before Peter King came in.

14th April 1940

Felt encouraged by increase of 8 in the number of communicants. We had 15 at Easter; the usual number is about 3–5. There are a nominal 1,000 on the station, but possibly only a third are off-duty and free to come at any time. Smalley has told me not to worry about numbers: "When they hear the first big bang and mess their pants, they'll come alright." Parade services at the AA sites seemed to go extra well. Wrote letters and saw Smalley about baseball kit. Visited guardroom cells where a man from 19 Squadron is under arrest awaiting court martial. A tough guy, and I could do nothing with him except to offer help.

What can one do? He didn't want to talk and in reply to friendly (as I thought) questions would say little more than "yes" or "no". Visited the mortuary and decided it must be altered. It's a disgraceful place. One can't let parents visit their dead there, though I don't want them to, in what is a dissecting room. The grim, stained table can't be moved out of sight.

Watched football match and talked to airmen. Went to Gas Defence centre where a corporal on duty wanted me. Inevitable question re banns or special licence. But any reason better than none for an introduction.

Oh yes, yesterday two airmen to see me about baseball. And in the afternoon, a long session with an airman, Blunden, who comes regularly to church, who needed to let off steam. Just listened and he said he felt better. He is half South American and a very good Christian.

Terrific flap this morning. Preparedness for everyone at dawn. One squadron took off on patrol. Nothing happened. Minor flaps have continued all day, for there have been unidentified aircraft flying near. Wellingtons flew over this afternoon showing their secret T device. In a raid on Stavangar this week we lost ten of them. That's about a whole squadron. Not a word about this in the press where all is presented in rosy hues.

Bigger congregation at evensong. Went to Red Lion with Major Smalley and K.K.Horn (Squadron Leader Ops). After supper talked to pilots I don't know so well and then finished the vintage port in the wellington boot with Nicky. We talked mainly about what I should do in the light of what Blunden told me yesterday when he let off steam. I am seeing him again tomorrow night. I didn't tell Nicky any names or least of all that the trouble is in his squadron (19).

15th April 1940

Varied morning round the camp. Most important job was arranging with Applee to have the dreadful mortuary changed. "De mortuary nil nisi bonum". I want a better table in it. It still has blood stains on it from Trenchard and Griffiths. Played squash in the afternoon with Ace Pace who, having lost one game, announced, "I shall now play with no regard for your safety." So he did. It is safer flying than playing squash with Ace. Al Williams is to be posted to Norway. Drew goes to Lossiemouth. This is a good thing, for though Drew is a pleasant person, they have not made an impressive pair of Flight Loots.

16th April 1940

What a day! Blunden to see me for most of the morning. It took a long time to get him to talk plainly and simply for he was very frightened. He went into details of what he had said earlier. He is being made to sign for an aircraft as being airworthy when he knows that it isn't. He is a fitter and the Flight Sergeant tells him to sign. It's very disturbing and ugly. He agrees to let me do something. The fitters and riggers believe that they will be put on a charge if they refuse to sign the airworthiness chit when ordered to by the Flight Sergeant; this particular instance is serious. The aircraft is Frankie Brinsden's Spitfire. He knows nothing of this. Fortunately I've got the confidence of Nicky, the adjutant, and I think we trust each other. So I went and told him what was happening but begged him to act without names coming up. I asked him bluntly, "Would you post a man away from here if I ask you to and tell you no more than that there is urgent cause?" He said he would. He asked nothing except the name, and the Flight Sergeant departed to a posting which at my hint had nothing to do with aircraft. The Flight Sergeant has gone, no reason given. The Spitfire has been rechecked.

Work on the plans for the new mortuary. Fussing as Mess officer. More attempts to get a pension for Wilson's mother. Many letters. Listened to Douglas Bader's very just complaints about the AOC's comments on his crash in the Spitfire. Bader now posted from 19 Squadron to 222 and so still with us. A good thing for 222. They need someone with his life and verve. Office session after tea and after supper. The rest of the day my own! But it's all lovely and the way I like it, and better still I'm going on leave tomorrow.

17th April 1940

After the Bible class I went across to the anteroom to find a party in full swing; 19 Squadron are going forward to Old Catton (used to be Horsham St Faith) tomorrow, for a fortnight. There is trouble ahead for here we are too full of aeroplanes. So I stayed but walked delicately till "Stevie" Stevenson, the "pocket battleship" CO of 19 Squadron, had left. He can't keep off tactics or cannons. He has no sense of humour. He is small, keen and a ball of fire. Party consisted of Robbie who has temporarily returned after appendicitis operation, Michael Lyne, Peter, John Baker, Gunning and Nicky (none of them of the type to listen to Stevie's lectures over a glass of gin on how to die for England.)

Eventually (and after Stevie had retired), Robbie was escorted to his room and put to bed. It was suddenly decided that Peter, who was sober for once, should also be put to bed. So he was after much rough and tumbling. When they had put him to bed without breaking any of King George's furniture and were leaving the room, he burst into tears. How thin is the crust! I hadn't taken part in the proceedings. Everyone except me had left the room when he broke. The last person in the world, you might think. He explained that he was tight; this was untrue. I tried to comfort him without much success; then I came over to my quarters feeling miserable. After all, it's a thing he would do himself to others, whether deserved or undeserved. It must have been done to him before. It's a symptom of the strain under which they are all living.

Turned up at breakfast from colour-hoisting parade in great form. Everyone full of gloom. Stevie, whose room is below Peter's, had been disturbed by the junketings and had sent for all those who were in the room last night. I was appealed to. I was in the room but it was admitted I had been entirely passive. However, Nicky, Stevie's adjutant, was involved; he is old enough to be Stevie's father. I said I would see Stevie before I went on leave. So I went to his office in the hangar – he's always there long before anything happens. I went in without Nicky having to announce me, and I began "Look ...". He listened. I felt I might have been explaining to a human being how some animals behave if they are under tension; and that tension produces different results in everyone. If he had everyone paraded before him, he would lower morale, increase tension, and make "something" out of what was a trivial incident even though it had kept him awake. To my relief and surprise he agreed with me. I said I would talk to those concerned (without saying to him that I had been in the room). With that I left him, went back to the anteroom and told them that all was well but that they must not do anything to keep the "pocket battleship" i.e. Stevie awake; he was too valuable for that. And with that I went on leave.

1st May 1940

Flew to Old Catton to see 19 Squadron, airmen and pilots. I spent the morning with the pilots who were at readiness. Douglas Bader came in from a patrol. He has been doing more than his share of patrols. He landed with his undercarriage up. We all saw it. The aircraft isn't very good; but he isn't hurt. He is flying on leave, so he strode with his parachute from the crashed aircraft to the Maggy in which he was going to fly to Duxford. He was still in a furious temper at landing with his wheels up, and all our soothing had no effect. He took his parachute, and flung it hard on the wing of the Maggy, saying "Fuck everything". The parachute went straight through the wing, making a lovely hole in it. So that was the second aircraft he had temporarily written off in an afternoon. But it restored his balance. Another aircraft was found, and he took off in that.

The flight came off readiness after lunch, so we went to our quarters at Old Catton which used to be the Group headquarters of bombers. I had been allotted the AOC's bedroom. John Petre and Nicky were waiting for us. In the evening we went to the Castle in Norwich, lots of beer before and after – "we" consisted of Nicky, John Baker and self. Mathieson and Peter joined us later; they had been kept at readiness for longer than the others. There we met Mr Bush. He told me that he was the owner of many night clubs in Norwich. He was well away, so well away that with only a modicum of encouragement he paid for our drinks for the evening, believing that we should get a commission for his son in the R.A.F. (Does he want him to die?) We drove back to Old Catton, after looking into a canal face to face. I thought Peter had been behaving in a very silly way with a female and I told him so, so firmly that, before I realised what was about to happen, he and John Baker had removed my trousers (decorum prevented them from removing my pants) and so to bed.

2ⁿᵈ *May 1940*

Peter flew me back to Duxford. He insisted on wearing a field service hat and, of course, since this is not designed for use in an open aircraft, it came adrift over Norwich and fluttered down. So I had to take over. My time on the Link trainer came in useful here, but as I refused to use the rudder, which I had not mastered on the Link – we flew level although kept going off course. The intercom was working one way only; he couldn't hear me; all I could hear was him singing "The Red Flag". Eventually he took over. We had a spot of low flying over the bombing range at Thetford, but even Peter was a bit shaken when a Wellington flew above us, without seeing us, and dropped a bomb which we could see coming down on us. We turned away somewhat sharply. When we got to Whittlesford we circled over Squadron Leader Copley's house because his daughter is alleged to be pretty; we turned too tightly and too long for my liking and then came into land here with a horrible side-slip landing. For all of which I bought him a half can of beer when we got to the Mess. It was a lovely flight, even though the cobwebs from last night and Mr Bush still linger. It was good to be with 19 Squadron again, airmen and pilots.

3ʳᵈ *May 1940*

The war, or the future of it, has got me down badly. I've been thinking over what Peter said to me yesterday after we had landed. He took up the trivial and broken ends of our conversation at Norwich. We walked out over the aerodrome for that is the only place where you can be private, if not safe. I talked to him about low flying; what I've experienced with him is mild compared to what he does in a Spit. I told him, plainly and, at the risk of wounding his esteem, that other pilots who like him thought he is doing things in the air for which he isn't good enough yet, and, even if he is good enough, are damn silly anyway. I talked about the girl at Norwich, the gist of what I said being that he isn't old enough to be stable yet, and that this piece, even from his own account, didn't sound extra hot. He accepted it all and replied in a very depressed way: "What does it matter? I shall be killed anyway; if not killed, I shall be maimed; there won't be much left to live with, and no job to go to after the end of the war. What kind of experience is this for taking a job and settling down?"

He said the R.A.F. would contract when the war was over; there would be no future for him there. So why not grasp some experience of something, anything, while there is a short time left? We talked and walked for a long time, very frankly and about many things with a directness that I never wanted to talk to any young man about. It clouded over the impression of wonderful weather at Old Catton, the spring and the distant hopes. Hanging over everything is the threat of the ominous and immediate future. We both of us smelled death. So he feels the hurry to do things while there is time, and before they go or he goes. Love and life are flying away. Life at Old Catton and here is "Beer today and gone tomorrow." 19 is a good squadron and I am fond of them all, but, oh, to have known them and their prestige and pride in the days of peace when there wasn't any hurry because death wasn't near.

5ᵗʰ May 1940

Service at the AA site cancelled because of panic. The other AA site is closed because we are short of guns and the gun has gone to Norway. Talked to airmen off-duty on the domestic side of the station; some were sun bathing; others were manning machine guns; some were doing both. Bader invited me to go to Old Catton in the Master to visit the squadron again. He wanted to show me what flying in "a real aircraft" was like. But after lunch, as soon as we got to the dispersal point, we found the Master was U/S; so was the Maggy. So instead I toured the machine gun sites, 222 Squadron dispersal points and talked to the men. Mathie and Michael Lyne came for tea.

Blunden came over to see me in the evening. He had flown over from Old Catton. The signing trouble was all cleared up. I knew this but he hadn't realised it. He stayed and talked. He praised Peter to the skies as a pilot and as an officer who looks after his men. This latter quality is not common now in the R.A.F.. I went out to the flare path till the early hours. Bits of excitement and very cold.

6th *May 1940*

The lance corporal who looks after our brigadier who looks after our defences said to me today apropos of nothing: "I hope you don't think I don't come to your services because I despise them. I am a Jew." In the evening I went with "Happy Laughing" Bassett of 222 Squadron to the Red Lion. He is an RC. He is feeling much shaken after his crash. He isn't fit to fly yet and has nothing to do here. I hope I cheered him up. Anyway he lived up to his nickname, so perhaps I succeeded. Now that 19 Squadron has gone forward, he stands out as more intelligent than the ordinary run of chaps, though the others aren't dim.

7th *May 1940*

Inspected the NAAFI stores this morning to find out if there were any goods we could buy for the Officers Mess. The retail prices are too high for us. Sidelights here and there make me think that there is an unbreakable racket within the NAAFI.

A Defiant with the new squadron leader and herald of the new squadron (all very secret indeed) arrived here this morning. CO's name is Hunter. I spent a long time going over it with the air gunner. The intensely secret part of it all is that it looks like a conventional fighter from the air, but it carries an air gunner who can shoot forward and backward, as well as the fighter guns. We suppose that the Germans don't know that we have any aircraft like this. It has come here because of the battles that are expected to come later this month. I like the gadgets which prevent the air gunner from shooting his own air crew. I can just squeeze into the air gunner's turret.

In the afternoon I spent a long time making my petrol wangle honest and to come within AMOs. Sat outside 19 Squadron hangar and talked to the airmen who were sunbathing as they waited for something to happen. Some of them seemed to be square pegs in round holes, with talents wasted. I have got several jobs to last me for a while. It's easier than ever before to talk to the airmen. They have lost their shyness. And they come up and chat of their own accord. This is what I wanted.

9th May 1940

Prepared address in morning. Went round the aerodrome and talked to all and sundry who were about. Nicky has come back from Old Catton. He is no longer adjutant of 19 Squadron; this is bad for 19, for he has been a good adjutant if at times a bit pompous. But he has earned promotion and is still with us in the Ops room.

Bob Oxspring has been posted to Norway. The signal came yesterday. I took him to Cambridge to the flicks but we were recalled and he was away by 7 p.m. I am sorry. He is good and solid, as you would expect of the son of a Sheffield steel manufacturer. He played a good game of squash; he talked; and how if and when he is killed (as he will be if he goes to Norway) he won't bullshit (as someone said to me of him).

Went out to the flare path yesterday evening and saw the mysterious "aircraft" doing tight turns in the beams of the searchlight – the fixed beam not the other beams. I came back and confirmed that I'd seen what others had seen by the Chance light. Story received with polite interest; both Woody and the Ops room said I must have been drinking. This is disrespectful and untrue. Corporal Colquhoun saw them and so did the ACs. Shall go again this evening if possible to see what may be seen. When I got back to the Mess at midnight late, I found everyone in deepest gloom over Churchill's speech. We have been warned. People outside the R.A.F. believe that if the Luftwaffe comes, we shall throw all our fighters in the air and fight and fight and fight. So we shall, but we haven't enough pilots or aircraft to make any difference. They don't know that. One or two of the watch coming from the Ops room seemed really scared. So with an apprehensive eye on the sky I went uneasily to bed.

10th May 1940

Germany invaded Belgium and Holland. The whole station and, I expect, the R.A.F. is in a flap. However, the station warrant officer said to me this morning as I walked over to the ops side, "From all this panic, sir, you might think the bloody Germans were in the next field already." The machine gunners are being trained in musketry, though there aren't enough rifles for them. The dug-outs are being pumped free of water. A most secret order from air ministry tells us how to make pikestaffs from sharp knives, presumably to stick up the backsides of the parachutists when they land; and of course they won't be firing on us when they come down! A pleasant message from Churchill which says, "Why not take one with you when you go?" It makes me laugh like a drain even though I don't want to go, but it has sobered some.

I was with Douglas Bader, his wife and sister in law, "setting things out" in the Ladies Room when the order came for 222 Squadron to leave at once for Digby. So that for the moment is good bye to Douglas who is one of the bravest men I have ever met and one of the most cheerful. He will be an immense loss to us all on the station, because of his courage, his cheerfulness; the example of his two wooden legs has kept us all up to the mark. When we first met, he used to say, "Sorry, Padre" every time he said "bloody"; this was every other word. I bore this for a while; then I started saying, "Bother! Sorry, Douglas." Things became easier. When he called me a "God botherer", I replied that his lack of attachment to institutional Christianity probably bothered God more than even I did. After that we were friends and talked. Playing squash with him was an experience; he can't move fast because of his two wooden legs; but he stands in the centre of the court and leaves you to run round him.

All leave has been stopped; no passes whatsoever; everyone to live on the station. 222 Squadron left at 4 p.m. The Defiants moved in at once – 246 with Philip Hunter. Everyone is very tense and apprehensive. This evening I went down to the Red Lion with Rupert Leigh who has come to be a tower of strength and flippant courage, and we dissolved the tension in rye and dry.

11th May 1940

Signal has come to Peter King who is acting adjutant of 66 Squadron to say that Heath is missing, believed killed over Norway. He left us last week. It's what he wanted, and I think he even wanted to be killed fighting for an invaded country. He was very upset because he wasn't accepted as a volunteer for Finland. God rest his soul. His death will be a blow to his fiancée whom I met. I tried to sort things out for them, but there wasn't much chance. With Heath, ideas and ideals came second to marriage. After the war he wanted to tour the world to find out what people really wanted to enable them to live in peace. I wish more of them thought like that besides being brave.

Applee has returned from duty at Old Catton. Peter is doing some mad flying and taking the most foolish risks. He is given three months to live. I must try and tick him off before the three months are up. It's such a damned silly death for a good pilot who knows better. But Yorkshire people are very obstinate.

Hell of flap this evening. At 9.30 p.m. it was reported that "they" were coming in by the hundred over Yarmouth. The Mess emptied in a minute and beer was left unfinished. The MO and I went to 66 dispersal point. In 15 minutes everything was called off. A false alarm.

12th May 1940

Our squadrons have been in action. 66 and 264 went to The Hague.

They got back in time for a late tea, having shot down two Germans. I met the Spits when they landed. Modest evening party in the Red Lion.

13th May 1940

Another raid by us over Holland. Gillies and Smith (66 and 264 Squadrons) are just back. Five Germans shot down, including two dive bombers. Everyone safe in 66; Peter King has landed at Calais; Browne at Le Zoute. So it's a good start to the morning's work.

It has been a curious day. 66 Squadron are rightly pleased with themselves. But there are long faces and a quiet manner in 264; there was no news of one section until 7.30 p.m. when one of them returned. Peter came in a Spit that needed servicing. He promptly got a bullshitting from Nicky and Applee, public in the Mess, and a private one from me about silly flying. I got T.T. injections this morning so one arm is U/S. I got Peter to drive me to Cambridge where we had tea with darling

Thel. Back here by 4.15 p.m. and Peter returned to Old Catton.

A Spit beat up the station just after we got back. The SMO and I guessed it was Peter King so we went out to dispersal point. Only one bullet hole in his aircraft. He had left Martlesham at 4 a.m., shot up The Hague (his words), shot an air gunner and killed him but didn't shoot down a plane. Flew to Calais; got there at 7 a.m. for breakfast and so back here. John Petre (who shouldn't be asked to kill anyone) who shot down an ME last week and killed the air gunner, told me all about this over dinner. He had a narrow escape; his plane was badly hit about; he landed with no oil pressure and no petrol. Things are getting very "Dawn Patrol". King said that Calais aerodrome was bombed and French planes destroyed. The terrific explosion which shook us last night at 1.30 a.m. was caused by a Wellington at Bassingbourn: the engine cut on taking off.

No one hurt, unlike one of the crew of a Wellington at Newmarket: he's been saved but both of his hands are burned off. The AOC has visited us to congratulate the pilots. But who remembers the widows and orphans and mothers, ours and German? My cheers are genuine enough but tempered by prayers for them. Our losses during the last few days have been terrific.

14ᵗʰ May 1940

Still no news of the five Defiants which are missing. One other returned last night after landing in Belgium to refuel. Feeling a bit poorly after another injection. Went across to look at two Wellingtons, a new type of Hurricane and a Mentor. Our two squadrons were sent off to The Hague this evening but recalled while at sea.

15ᵗʰ May 1940

Two more Defiant survivors have come back, one pilot and his air gunner. This makes a loss of five machines and eight men. These two men were shot down in flames by MEs over a Dutch canal. They bailed out, borrowed clothes from a farm and walked to The Hague. The US ambassador gave them a car and a revolver and told them where a destroyer was embarking refugees. They reached it a few minutes before it sailed. They were flown from Hawkinge this morning.

I've drawn a gun and ammunition from 19 Squadron armoury. This is a wangle and contrary to the Geneva Convention. But as the war is now being run, I don't think that German parachutists will respect that convention on a dark night when they can't see what I am. As parachutists are alleged to be disguised as clergymen, I don't want to be shot by one of our own guards without a fight, either.

16ᵗʰ *May 1940*

A Whitley landed here en route home after bombing petrol dumps in the Ruhr. Went and talked to the pilot. 150 aircraft went on the raid. This one dropped all its cargo – 35cwt – at once! Went inside – there seems to be more room than in a Wellington.

Went to 66 Squadron dispersal at 3 p.m. to say goodbye; they go to Old Catton and later to Coltishall. Unless they are bombed out we shan't see them again. It wasn't a particularly cheerful occasion. Campbell-Colquhoun and others did some *feux de joies* and a certain amount of damage with their revolver firing. I was just leaving when Lucky Leigh and some others came up to say goodbye. It wasn't very easy. 66 Squadron hasn't been as easy to know as 19; Peter King, Rimmer (no more imitations of Chamberlain and Churchill – considered almost a blasphemy), Kennard and Smith, I shall miss, and especially Peter King who made his mark here. So off they went and returned flying over us in tight squadron formation; all finely done. Dr Browne took me home on his pillion – an epic ride as we were both fairly new to motor cycling. We returned here just in time to see 19 returning and flying with a most exciting piece of squadron formation. So with 19 back we are ourselves again though not so much ourselves as before without 66 and Billy Burton. I wish all those boys could come through the war, and Lucky Leigh. The world would be a duller place without Rupert Leigh. In the short time we've known

Pilots of No. 66 Squadron, including Flying Officer Reginald Rimmer, Flight Sergeant Jones, Pilot Officer 'Bobby' Oxspring and Flying Officer George Brown, in the squadron crew-room in early 1940. Rimmer was killed in September 1940, age 21. HU 59071

each other I think we developed a high mutual respect. The picnic that Peter King was to have given for his fiancée, Thel and me, will have to wait for happier days in this world or the next.

19ᵗʰ May 1940

I've been spending most of the past two days at the dispersal points where the airmen and pilots are for most of the day and night. It's not easy to find amusements for them. Sunbathing yesterday with Applee who said, "Jews always suffer most in a war so that's why I got into the R.A.F. as soon as I could." Wellingtons and Whitleys coming back from Germany continue to land here. One bomb aimer told me that as he pulled the lever he shouted, "No bloody pamphlets this time". Two more Defiant aircrew have turned up, leaving two still lost, including Skelton the Flight Lieutenant who is such a good talker and intelligent. One of these boys returned on a ship packed with refugees and was machine gunned on the deck. Went to Cambridge and had supper with Thel. It was lovely and so happy. Went to the Sergeants Mess on return and found the Group Captain there, so stayed with him. He left at 11 p.m. and Peter and Logical Lyne turned up to say goodbye to Flight Sergeant Low and Warrant Officer Berry who are both rather pals of mine. A real Sergeants Mess drinking party ensued and only ended at 1 a.m. with Peter looking as full of beer as a barrel. Woke up this morning as fresh as a daisy. Are they fresh?

20ᵗʰ May 1940

Sunbathing yesterday afternoon outside the "Vicarage" when Mathie hurried up and asked me to lend him the Hillman. 19 has been ordered to France and at short notice. He has a girl in Cambridge. This and the war news, which is far worse than anything in the papers, has cast gloom. I can't bear to think of these boys being shot down as most of them will be. They have been so good to me and helped me so much from my first raw and shy appearance in their world. Went to the Sergeants Mess and talked to the 19 pilots. Then came back to our Mess. Peter asked if he might come and talk. We had a long conversation about dying, about not having much time to live, about the next world, about oneself in this world, about not caring what other people think. It was a grim conversation which disturbed me very much though I don't think I showed it. I could hardly have it so freely and agonisingly frank with anyone else. How many will come back? Which ones? All one's prayers can't keep them in the sky.

It is difficult to keep the Christian hope and the faith in the little change between the two lives. Peter and I talked long about this, and how death didn't matter. But it does matter. I am thankful to be trying to do something as a priest, but that it should be telling young men of twenty, real good young men – and Peter isn't the only one who asks and talks – how to die, and why there is nothing to be afraid of (except the pain which we don't mention). I am not to let this get me down. I am to be the cheerful one on the station. Say my prayers. Germans evidently busy again in Belgium for they have got a standing patrol of their aircraft 60 miles off Harwich.

The fighter pilots are a physical and mental type. They must be short, rather than tall; otherwise they could hardly get into a Spit or a Hurricane. They must react extremely quickly. So they are fiery and explosively high-spirited. In these conditions they tend to live violently and enjoy themselves violently, for everything may be the last time. They tend to talk quickly; and you have to talk quickly back to them.

22ⁿᵈ May 1940

Peter and I went to have dinner in Cambridge with Thel. Called en route at the Unicorn at Trumpington for cider, "for immediate internal use". Then beer at the Prince Regent in Regent Street and a wonderful evening at home. Peter recited "The Green Eye of the Little Yellow God" and sang "The Red Flag" and "The Internationale" to our records. A phone call from the station sent us hurrying back at midnight. There was a flap which lasted all night. The Germans are now at Abbeville, so it's unlikely that 19 Squadron will go to France.

Thank God for last night. It was a break in the midst of this dreadful anxiety and gloom. It's such an effort to keep cheerful and appear decently carefree and not over-anxious. I fear there is far worse to come; so do other people but only people like Smalley and Woody and mention it and out of hearing of aircrew. Peter has been talking today – there's nothing for 19 to do but wait – about not wanting to die yet. He wants more from life than he fears he will have time to get. He said, "War is all tears". You wake up in the morning; for an instant the horrors have been forgotten, and then slowly they crowd in as consciousness returns. War, mud, blood and tears. One isn't afraid of dying. The heartache is to see these young men waiting to have their lives cut short. While they wait there's nothing much for them to do. They talk to me. Thank God for yesterday evening with Thel. There has been laughter and carefreeness for a while.

24th May 1940

The tension and anxiety continue. We all realise what seems to be coming inevitably, none more so than the pilots. One hopes to contrive to keep them cheerful. They are getting tired, too little sleep, too much waiting, too much strain. Bombers landing here at night and other alarms don't make for good nights. 264 Squadron went over Boulogne yesterday; it's in German hands. They have gone off again today. The Assistant Chaplain-in-Chief, Cox of Halton, came to see me yesterday. He is a good man and a tremendous encouragement.

(I met him later at Gibraltar and he told me he had come to see me for two reasons: first, to make sure that my morale wasn't cracking and to see if I needed cheering up; and second, to try and show that he understood what life might be like at Duxford. I know also that my cynicism on one occasion made one humourless intelligence officer wonder whether my morale was cracking, for I said at breakfast one morning after an unusually disturbed night, "Wouldn't it be better if we just went and lived in the fields and asked the Germans to come here without so much noise?")

Oh, for an end so that we could have more time to play and no cause to think about what may come? We, and by "we" I mean those of us who are called "chairborne" as distinct from the airborne R.A.F., have been warned that the outlook is as unpleasant for us as for the pilots. But there was no need to say this, except perhaps for the sake of the dim few who think that we can win without aircraft.

25th May 1940

19 Squadron have left for Hornchurch which is nearer the Belgian and French coasts so that they can cover the evacuation. Went to Cambridge for an hour to see Thelma; I couldn't properly be away longer than this. Peter wanted to come with me and say goodbye, but there was no time. Returned to take Clouston, John Baker, John Petre and Peter in my car to dispersal point. I saw them off. Conversation difficult when people are wearing oxygen masks; however, I gave Peter's aircraft a strong twitch on the rudder which is as good as a slap on the back, owing to the pressure on the "stick". Not a cheerful event. However, they seemed to appreciate my being there. I was saying goodbye to very well-known friends.

92 Squadron have come in to replace 19.

26th May 1940

19 Squadron have shot down ten. The Hornchurch wing has shot down 40 in all off the Belgian coast. Sinclair, Stevie, Peter and one other are missing. Too numb to feel much; all one can do is to pray off and on all day. We are preparing for an invasion. 20 parachutists over Dover last night – killed before they landed. No further news of Peter and the others. They went up before breakfast towards the French coast and met about 30 Ju's. They fell for the usual German trick, for above them MEs were waiting. It's said that Peter and Michael Lyne got a German each. We are here all depressed and anxious about these casualties.

9.30 p.m. Rather more hopeful news. Sinclair has landed at Manston. A Sergeant Pilot is in a French hospital. Logical Lyne is wounded and landed on Margate beach. He is at Deal Hospital. (The nurse tried to remove his trousers on the beach in order to dress his wound, but he resisted this.) Peter was last seen baling out over the Channel near the French coast; there is a chance he was picked up. Stevie was last seen flying towards Germany. Ball is wounded in the head.

This has been a black and anxious Sunday: I wish I could pray as I sleep. What night thoughts for the twentieth century! Goodbye to Peter, returned with a smart salute from the cockpit; and last talk at dispersal about seeing Thel and having dinner next week. Tonight you don't know whether he is alive or not. It sounds so easy to say, "He bailed out over the sea". But have you ever seen the inside of a Spit? Imagine bailing out of that, with the wind resistance, at 250 mph at the slowest! And then – he is a good swimmer. I go on saying prayers – I do for all my friends, and he is – was – one of the most loyal; but where does the prayer reach him? Whether in the flesh or the spirit I cannot say, to adapt St Paul. This day last week we were sitting here talking about dying and was trying to explain how the Christian faith made it easier, what prayer did, how the good things we love are imperishable. He talked again about it and quoted me to myself, notably on the drive back from Thel when we were suddenly recalled. So he took it all in.

27th May 1940

The Defiants have been over Dunkirk and Boulogue and shot down five plus two possibles. No one hurt. One man had a bullet in his petrol tank. The sides were scorched by heat but there was no fire. Lucky Leigh and I met them at dispersal.

Latest news given me about Peter by the Wing Commander Ops at 9.30 a.m. this morning. He was last seen swimming strongly towards the shore near Calais. He was half a mile off shore. There were small boats near. People in the Mess have been asking for news, singing his praises and "bounce". Found rather a grim joke by Peter this morning. The ration demand had been signed by him. As I was counter-signing duplicates this morning I noticed also that the demands for a day last week had evidently been signed by someone else; I assumed someone authorised would sign them if I didn't or couldn't. These also were signed "P.V. Watson, P/O." The day was one on which he had a wonderful hangover and was still happily the worse for wear when he woke up. No doubt this morning's signature had been put in to draw a solemn rebuke from me. But there is no one to laugh with.

Michael Lyne has a shattered knee. It is thought he may not fly again.

Before going to bed last night I read the chapter in Ecclesiastes "Remember now thy creator ..." It turned up by chance. What a terrible qualification there is: "... while the evil days come not nor the years draw night when thou shalt have no pleasure in them." A false commentary on our young men. There is a further call for pilots, air observers and air gunners. The position is described as increasingly grave. I'm knocked out by the second inoculation and am going to sleep hoping that the bombers won't come tonight. The usual question – where is Bob? Where is Gerald? "When they shall be afraid of that which is nigh."

28th May 1940

Terrific explosion in the night shook the windows and house. Bassingbourn was being bombed. It turns out that the bomber was one of ours from Ripon. He thought he was bombing Flushing. He went on to Snowdon and bombed that also! The Belgian Army and the King surrendered.

264 Squadron have been in action again: five shot down but three Defiants are missing. Spoke to Peter Howard Williams (of 19 Squadron) on the aerodrome. He had come from Hornchurch. No one hopeful about Peter, but too soon yet to be sure.

Sergeant Steer shot down an ME this morning in flames. He told me he could see the pilot struggling in the cockpit to get out. He couldn't. Steer was sick in his own cockpit.

Pilots of the 'Duxford Wing' relax with drinks at Fowlmere. In the middle, with a moustache, is Harry Steere, who was decorated for bravery before the Battle began. He was killed in 1944, age 30. CH 1370

29th May 1940

A day of mixed feelings. The afternoon well spent in Cambridge in getting a steel helmet and trying to get a revolver licence and a revolver. 264 Squadron have shot down 35 German planes today. Great exultation. They were badly shot up but no one crashed. One air gunner bailed out, but why is not yet known. 264 are expected here tomorrow. Yesterday they lost Hatfield, the Canadian A/G officer, who was friendly with me and reminded me of "Canada" Reid of Lancing. No further news of Peter or Stevie. We are beginning to think there is no further reason to hope, particularly for Peter. We should have had news by now if he had been picked up near Calais. If he wasn't picked up, one hopes that in the mercy of God he was mortally wounded or killed outright. Oh God, to think that I should write this. There are so many things I want to remember about him and nothing to forget. In the Mess one still instinctively looks to see if he is there to see a joke, or one begins to embroider an incident to tell him, or to ask a question and receive the lowdown on a service obscurity. I must write tomorrow to his people and to Stevie's. One still prays for both of them. It's an odd prayer: "God bless them and keep them from harm. Deliver them from evil wherever in the universe they may be."

My own feelings aren't made easier when members of the Mess lament: "What a good officer! What a companion!" Thank God we "tired the sun with talking" often enough about the final things. At least I feel I have been useful to one brave young man. I have done something and learned a lot. The silly little things are badly missed – the baitings to make me call him or someone "a nasty, shitty type", the super-respectful "sirs" and deference in the anteroom. "I'm not fussy" is his motto. It's a good one and typical. I write "is" – because I must as a Christian. "Was" won't be true.

I hope that the Germans have understood that 264 have not returned to us tonight. We are promised bombs, airborne invasion and tank-carrying aircraft. Perhaps those who die earliest are the lucky ones. Perhaps it is true that those whom the gods love die young.

31st May 1940

264 Squadron returned victorious yesterday. Sixty planes shot down in three days. I went to meet them at dispersal point and talked a lot to King, the remarkable air gunner. The boys were very tired but *exalté*. Terrible descriptions of the bombing of Dunkirk and of our transports. Poor B.E.F. The slaughter must have been ghastly. Our satellite aerodrome, G1 or Fowlmere, used yesterday for the first time.

Went to the Ops room at 4 p.m. and again at 8.30 p.m. to watch our bombers going out (on the board). Wrote to Peter's father and mother. Went through his possessions; sealed up his letters and papers. These are harmless but will be destroyed if he doesn't return. A little hope for three pilots have landed at Dover who were picked up from the Channel. It was a painful business with the letters: there was one telling him to report for flying instruction; there were uniform catalogues, FTS bills and the final Duxford Mess bill.

Signposts taken down from the roads; the barricades are going up at the cross roads and elsewhere.

2nd June 1940

Budd, the adjutant of 19 Squadron, and I went to see Stevie's people at Holme Hale, 18 miles the other side of Thetford. No sign posts; frequent and searching examinations by guards; road obstructions. The journey was slow and eventful. On the return we had two pints at Barton Mills and felt better. It was an unhappy business. We picked up Thel and dined at the Trumpington Red Lion.

3rd June 1940

66 Squadron turned up this evening. I put up Peter King and Campbell in my quarters. Peter had my bed and Campbell had Pingo's old room next door. I made do quite comfortably with a combination of the sofa and the arm chair. The Tannoy and the phone kept going all night. Both boys were up at 4 a.m. and flew off at 5 a.m. Told Peter K about Peter; they were great friends. All Peter K said was: "My God! That's made me angry about them getting Watty. Leave it to me, and I'll get an extra one for Watty's sake." It won't do any good, but it helped the feelings. It's now assumed that there is no hope for either Peter or Stevie. I said a requiem for them both this morning at about the time that they went down last Sunday, and also for 66 Squadron, 92 and 19 who were on ops this morning. I had in mind the verse in the psalms "Though I take the wings of the morning and remain in the uttermost parts of the sea, there also shalt thy hand find me."

Bit of a party at the Red Lion this evening for 66. Lucky Leigh was much in evidence with his "sharp pints of beer". 66 and 92 returned this morning. There were no casualties; they shot down 30 planes between them. I saw them come in. It is an exciting and ghastly business. Slept this afternoon.

4th June 1940

66 Squadron turned up again last night. Peter King was billeted on me in the small hours. The camp commandant from Old Catton came in and out of kindness of heart asked for news about Peter. He went on to say how much Peter had enjoyed my last visit to Old Catton. It does hurt so much. The only thing to do is to work hard on this station where there are so many reminders of him. One still turns or waits for him to come into the anteroom. I've never known anyone yet with so much candour and honesty and so few reservations. Towards the end he seemed to shed any reservations and we were friends that might have known each other for years. The difference in age made little odds.

"I'm not fussy" is one thing I want to remember; and also the scene the last time he was in the Sergeants Mess with Michael Lyne and myself. He had rows of glasses of sludge, full and empty, before him. He was drinking his way through them, looking like Toby Belch, with tunic unbuttoned and trousers unbuttoned some way down because he thought he was full of beer – as he was. That was a grand scene.

No news of Sergeant Irwin. He must have been killed at the same time that Peter went down. Neither would have been lonely on arrival.

Hunter, the CO of 264 Squadron, has been awarded the DSO and Cookie the DFC. May both live to get the medals.

5th June 1940

Went up in a Defiant in the air gunner's seat. A lovely day for it, all sun and no cloud. We saw 19 coming home below us. They flashed by and we turned to follow them over Cambridge and then watched from above as they beat up the aerodrome. We were up for half an hour. It was a lovely, thrilling time though not very comfortable. I am too large for the turret. I was much too nervous to move it about. Getting out in a hurry must be uncomfortable. But how hard for the gunners fighting in those cramped boxes.

Frankie Brinsden has told me about Peter. The action took place early on Sunday morning. He was shot down at 8 a.m. A cannon shell hit his aircraft. He seemed to be some time getting out. The aircraft was on fire. He was seen to float down with his chute open. There was no doubt as to his identity, for he was wearing his favourite black overalls, the only pilot to have them. It is most probable that he was very badly wounded when the plane was hit. The sea was black with oil. French and Germans were shooting those who parachuted. The Germans were taking no prisoners. One takes refuge in the likely hope that he was badly wounded enough to be unconscious before he reached the water. Stevie was seen spinning out of control over German territory.

It is good to have 19 Squadron here again; but one recalls the lines:

> Remember those who came not back from the war,
> The bowed heads, the veiled faces.

A nice letter has come from Mrs Watson. They cling to hope. I must write and tell them gently not to hope any more. Peter showed me the ropes of the R.A.F. and didn't allow me to feel too strange. I told him that there was no need to feel sorry for the dead, that dying was not a lonely business, that the real life, where he would have the fullness of the good things he loved here and had so little time to enjoy or work for, started when this life ended. Once again one will learn from him. But it's a heavy business at times here, and lightened by being able to say thank you to God for knowing him.

If you have seen the inside of a Spitfire, you will know how it could become hell on earth or in the sky. Imagine trying to escape from the cockpit, wounded, and the plane doing over 300 mph. People are calling them "knights" and it's just. They are the bravest of the brave. Thank God to have known so well a very *"parfit gentle"* one. He has made one's own life so much happier and richer. One thing I will try not to be and that is sentimental. That would quickly draw – in a Yorkshire accent – the rebuke of "bullshitting".

John Baker has confirmed Frankie's account of Peter. He was hit in the side of the cockpit by a cannon shell from a ME 109. He was on the tail of another ME and had shot down a Ju 87. He came down in the sea off Calais harbour. I wonder how he managed to pull himself out of the cockpit. He can't have lived very long.

6th *June 1940*

Dismal day. Air raid last night: 12 incendiary bombs dropped over Thriplow (in a search for our satellite aerodrome). No harm done. Peter's kit has arrived from Hornchurch and the last business has been completed. The things were very personal: letters and photos, a skull cap or rugger cap souvenir from school, and other precious things he took with him, my letter reminding him he owed me 6s 6d and asking him for Thel to come and spend his May 48 hours leave with us, his blue pyjamas which were very "special". I have kept the English dictionary, a very small one, which he used at school and which he took everywhere with him; he read it before going to sleep. One looks forward to another greeting and to having the strangeness taken off another new life. I'd no idea that anyone whom I'd known for only four months could leave a hole.

Lucky Leigh and others have just come into the room (midnight); they claim to have made a perfect night interception without seeing the raider.

Dimmy has died. He was shot down in flames over Folkestone 48 hours ago and seemed to be doing well. He had by most standards lived an unlovely life.

7th *June 1940*

We were coming back to our quarters last night, we being Copley, "Ming" Carter, Nicholls and myself, when an enemy aircraft with its lights on came over. A few minutes later Lucky Leigh and three others came in flying in such tight formation that at one moment all their lights looked like one aircraft. It was, as he would say, "amazing". No connection between the two incidents above. From midnight onwards there were raids; nothing very near us, though rumour says the raid was at Upworth where an AC was killed. We had fighters up and had to keep the flare path lit all night.

Conference with the AOC here to point out the futility of sending up Spits at night. Leigh told me that you can't take your eyes off the night flying instruments for more than a few seconds. However accurate the "vector", the Spits can't do much at night fighting. This was news to the AOC.

If we had no planes up at night and no lights on, we should be peaceful because we should be invisible except when stray bombers wanted to land. A Defiant cracked up near Linton this morning. Carnaby and his air gunner bailed out but landed safely despite being fired on by the Home Guard. Vicar of Pampisford, Punchard, came and talked for two hours. It was a change and I was able to talk freely to someone about some parts of my job.

Most of the morning, except for Punchard, and all the afternoon, have been spent in dealing with the missing from 19 and 264 Squadrons, and their relatives. In one way and another, by local events and the general news, the war is getting grimmer and grimmer. Most of us will go to bed hence forwards rather uneasily. I don't mind that so much as losing friends and watching the others get more and more tired:

> Father who endest all
> Pity our broken sleep.
> For we lie down with tears
> And waken but to weep.

8th June 1940

Thel's birthday. Air raids starting at 11 p.m. last night and lasting all night. Nothing nearer here than Mildenhall and Cottesmore which has been badly damaged. Stokes was sent up but fortunately landed after the first all clear. The second alarm was at 3 a.m. but I was asleep.

Hotter weather than ever; letter to me from one of Peter's girls.

10th June 1940

The German that bombed Upwood gave the letter of the day when challenged. The flare path was lit accordingly and Upwood was bombed.

Wrote yesterday to next of kin, including Mrs Watson. Spoke with Browne and Applee (the MOs about John Baker. He has landed a Spit with the undercart up. The AOC wants to blow him, court martial and the lot. This would finish him mentally as a pilot. Better advice has been followed: John has been sent on a week's leave instead. Peter told me on the way to Old Catton recently that what John wanted was a friend. He did his best. I have been told that I must have a try and do what I can for him when he comes back from leave.

Went up in a Maggy with Sutherland (19 Squadron) to get cool. Odd not to see Peter's head in front. We went to Bassingbourn to inspect the "friendly" bomb craters, and then to Audley End. Took photographs. The second time we took off, Sutherland forgot about his flaps and so we just, but only just, staggered into the air.

Lucky Leigh told me that Iris R/T was being deliberately jammed by dance music, the same record being repeated. He called "Shut up" but not so nicely, whereupon the station increased its signal strength. Leigh thought the jamming came from this country.

Distracting and painful experience: I had a vivid dream about Peter. He seemed to be here again, and everything as usual. He was in a mood when he became fierce with conviction. Then I woke up and the dream in retrospect became a nightmare.

Went to Cambridge to have supper at the KP with Thel; took Sutherland. To the Pike and Eel for beer.

11th *June 1940*

Into Cambridge this morning to see Michael Williams back on 48 hours from Dunkirk.

Defiant crashed off the perimeter track this evening. I got there with the ambulance. Air gunner has a broken jaw but is otherwise alright. We could not find the pilot. We searched and found him at last hidden in the foam from the fire wagon and in the young corn. He was dead.

12th June 1940

Blunden came to see me last night. He was one of Peter's fitters at Hornchurch. The patrol took off about 5 a.m. Peter was strapped in and climbed out exclaiming that he must have a pee. He gave some letters to Blunden to destroy if he didn't come back. He took his tunic and forage cap with him. Very much himself, laughing and joking. Blunden returned Peter's respirator to me and his scarf (which I have kept). I felt unhappy again. Later in the evening 19 Squadron started a party in the Mess but it lacked kick; everyone was thinking too much about the absentees. Pinkham, the new CO of 19, managed to be the leading spirit; he is much more in Peter's line than Stevie. In the end everyone was gay enough externally. For the present these parties bring back too many thoughts. One isn't used yet to the absences and to the idea that the door won't open to bring Peter and the others in.

13th June 1940

News from Air Ministry that Stevie and Skelton are POWs. The latter is wounded and in a convent. Plans in the air for Stevie's escape. More or less serious suggestion that there should be a Pimpernel scheme – this from the new CO. I had to decline an invitation to share in it!

15th June 1940

Thel telephoned yesterday and I went for lunch. I read a letter from Mrs Emmett to say that Bob had been killed in action. There seems to be no more to be said. Thelma and I were both so fond of him. One feels numb with it all. Bob and Peter gone. It won't be lonely dying. I am too numb to write any more. There's nothing more to be said with both of them gone.

(I got to know Bob Emmett when I lived at Esher and we travelled to and from Waterloo daily. He taught me to play squash and for three years we played several times a week. In 1960 when I was in the Lewes

County Library I picked up by chance a history of the East Surrey Regt and learned more. He sailed for France on 5thApril 1940; he was in Brussels on 19th May, 1940. On 21st May his battalion, 116th, moved to protect Avelgem. The battalion sent out patrols across the demolished bridge over the Escaut at Ruggee. Bob was sent out alone to see what had happened to the first patrol, and in going he was shot by a sniper and killed.)

21st June 1940

Serious air raid on Tuesday. The aircraft was over here about midnight. We listened to it, standing outside the Mess. We watched the AA guns open and heard whistling incendiaries drop on Cambridge where about 11 people were killed by another large bomb. Petre, Clouston and Ball were sent up. Petre and Clouston claim one shot down apiece. Petre is badly burned but alive. The aircraft shot down by Ball came down near Fulbourne. I went to see it the next morning. The debris was scattered over 300 yards. There was some loot among it: rugger vests and bales of French cloth. Three prisoners are here with us: the navigator, von Arnim, was given breakfast in the Mess and I was given charge of entertaining him. A sergeant is in the guard room; one wounded officer is in the sick bay. We buried a corpse, Paul Gerech, assumed to be RC, at Whittlesford today, I represented the CO. It was strange to see the Nazi flag on the coffin in England. While I was looking at the wreckage, I was joined by the AOC of the Bomber Group; we both looked at the bales of cloth, then at each other, and said nothing.

Life is now very hectic. "Ted Kid Lewis", the boxing instructor here, is suspected of fifth column activity. I think he is merely punch drunk and talks, so he shouldn't be here. Croker, a corporal, is also suspect and is being watched by MI5. He knows this and came to see me and to get advice. Two undisturbed nights. But it looks as if there will be life tonight.

28ᵗʰ June 1940

I've been too busy or too sleepy to write. Many air raids but no immediate excitements. Went to London on Tuesday to see Michael Lyne in the Royal Masonic Hospital. He told me of the awful time they had at Deal when he was lying in a ward there and there was a raid. Yesterday I saw John Petre in hospital at Bury. He is badly burned and seems very low. Spent yesterday evening at G1 with 19 Squadron, talked with the men and later with the pilots. One missed Peter badly · and even more today for a situation arose – it's not worth recounting – in which his horse sense would have been invaluable. It was the kind of situation in which he was always able to offer the light advice. I miss them both so – Bob and Peter. Funny experience last night: the lights went out after I got into bed and could hear German aircraft. I put my uniform over my pyjamas. I needed something warm for my neck, and I could have sworn that someone – whether in the flesh or in the spirit, as St Paul would say, I do not know – said, "Take the scarf from the drawer". I had entirely forgotten I had Peter's long woollen one. I put it on and took courage in an "I'm not fussy" attitude. I am getting tired of these night interruptions.

4ᵗʰ July 1940

Played squash with John Baker and beat him. Our secret rocket defence was let off by accident. The specially trained corporal pressed the button in an idle moment, probably leaned his elbow on it. Up went, for all to see, a row of rockets with wires dangling on the end. The idea is that they rise to the height of raiders; the wires catch the props or wings and down come the planes.

Our intelligence officers have discovered a signal code book near the crashed aircraft shot down by John Petre. This is apparently just what we wanted.

The real attack on England and on the aerodromes is about to begin, so we are told. One expects the Germans in the next field any day now.

I copied these two poems from "Punch" yesterday:

No comrades can pursue him.
He has taken
A way not one of them has travelled on,
Leaving a sleeper who will not awaken
To say that he has gone.
Has he found distances beyond known heeding,
Scanning the illimitable with young keen eyes,
Maybe on errand as bravely urgently speeding
Through new uncharted skies?

There is no word of him for any knowing
So brave a glory so to pass away.
He knew the dawn, with it had his bright glory,
And elsewhere has his day.

***

God, give us grace that we
Flying our fighters to eternity
May, meteor like, before we fall
Leave fiery trails of light that all
Truth's sons may clutch, and clutching rise
To blast Hell's spawn from Heaven's skies.

The last line spoils it: it is by a Sergeant Pilot.

4ᵗʰ August 1940

Ian Sutherland was killed today at Northolt. He was flying in a
Blenheim when it nose-dived in. Nothing identifiable beyond a scrap
of paper with his name on it has been found. He was at Northolt on
a Spit course; he need not have been in a Blenheim.

He was nice indeed – Magdalen, Oxford at its best. I wish we could
have had more games of squash and pleasant times together. The crash
has added to our general heaviness of spirit.

The Czechoslovakian pilots of No. 310 Squadron. Centre, holding a book, is John Boulton. CH 1299

Bathed today at Byron's Pool with Boulton, the very elegant instructor of the Czech squadron which has joined us.

7th August 1940

Went with Budd to Halton for Ian's funeral. We arrived at Halton parish church in the nick of time. Spoke to his father and brother afterwards. Got back here at 2.30 p.m., boxing, and looked in at the dance band and talked with them about the change from a £15 a week job to 14 shillings with keep. Am seeing Carter about making them AC1s; this will help a little.

After supper with Nigel Browne (F.O. "whirling sprays") and Bergman (Czech squadron), to the Sawston Black Lion and then on to the Trumpington Unicorn until 10.30 p.m. Party here afterwards to say farewell to Grey, the signals officer. It lasted till 2 a.m. Browne,

Bergman, Lynch – who falls out of chairs for no visible reason – Grey and myself went for a walk when all the bottled beer was finished. We gave it up after being stopped by nervous sentries with fixed bayonets and fingers on triggers. Nearly fell into the "Decontam" building on the way back; talked here till well after 3 a.m.

8th August 1940

Colour-hoisting prayers this morning. Feeling very fit. Letters; lunch with Thel at the KP, and then I went to the G site at Caxton. Asked for a service on Sundays. Squash with Nigel Browne to get rid of any beer from last night.

16th August 1940

Back from leave yesterday. In the morning prepared talk for Sunday. Talked to Harper, the chaplain under training, who has been posted to me for what the pilots call "spiritual Link training". Later took him on a tour of the station. To G1: talked to station defence chap, Sussex regiment men and B flight – to the latter about their bombing at Eastchurch. Toured the pillboxes. A schizophrenic to see me: he wants to be an air gunner. Another man to see me about loan. 19 Squadron have shot down 3 off Felixstowe with their new canon. They met a raid of 150 which turned tail and fled at the sight of Spitfires.

17th August 1940

Met Nigel in Cambridge at 7.15 p.m. Supper at the Bath, beer ad lib or almost at the Mill near Little St Mary's. Talk about Cambridge (he was at Corpus), the law tripos and theology (he is a Presbyterian).

18th August 1940

Took services at the AA sites and G2. Letters after lunch; classical record concert in the hangar after tea. Air raid warning stopped evensong. 46 and 66 Squadrons came in this evening. Billeted a Canadian pilot from 66 in my room. Me on sofa.

19th August 1940

Four alarms today. Honnington, Coltishall and Newmarket were bombed. 19 Squadron in action this evening. Haines and Steere got one each, over the sea. Went to the flare path and watched Steere come in at G1. Heard from him how he had circled over Studd of 66 who had been shot down in the sea. Steere got boats to Studd but it was too late. He was drowned. He must have been wounded. I liked him. He gave me some pleasant games of squash. He was one of the better types in 66. He was immensely tall and too tall strictly to be a Spitfire pilot. I remember his drooping and bored figure when he first came here as a pilot after being PA to the AOC (Leigh Mallory).

21st August 1940

Disturbed morning due to air raid alarm. No hostile plane came over. The MO and I got the air conditioning plant working in sick bay (not least for our comfort). In afternoon visited queer woman in Whittlesford who wants to entertain the Czechs, but why? Squash with Watkins (Ops B). Church Army captain turned up about opening a hut. Evening with Major and Mrs Smalley. Early to bed.

22nd August 1940

Talk with CO about the party tomorrow, Friday. Another talk with

Church Army captain. Lunch with Thel. Then to K site where I was given a pot of wild honey! Evening at G1 with 19 Squadron.

23rd August 1940

Air raid at 9.30 a.m. Dornier came out of the clouds above us and prepared to take a run in. AA shot it down! Another warning at midday. In afternoon visited gun sites and got ready for party. Party went with a bang, and I put away many Rye and gingers. Met Neale, of the Royal Sussex: he is stationed at Wyton. Later had songs with the Czechs and they made us all wear our shirt tails out, with ties tied round as belts. Looked very smart and chic.

24th August 1940

Rather a headache this morning! Cox, the Assistant Chaplain-in-Chief from Halton, called with suggestions re mortuary. Went to Cambridge to see Thel; had to get special leave as there was flap on. But she was "busy" and I couldn't see her. Heard at 7 p.m. that she had had her baby at 7.15 p.m., a son. Kept here until 8.30 p.m., then went and drank my health with Wedd.

25th August 1940

Services at AA site and G2. Saw Thel on way through Cambridge. Inspected burial sites for us and wrote letters. Visited G1 in the afternoon, taking up library. Talked particularly with Lane and Brinsden and also with lots of airmen. In the evening went with Nigel to the Red Lion Grantchester and talked for two hours over one pint of beer (it can be done). We stopped on the way back and were told of a purple warning; we had eight miles in inky darkness with only our side lights. Took 50 minutes. Germans looking for us during the night but dropped bombs on Cambridge instead.

26th August 1940

Colour-hoisting parade. Looked for parcel of comforts lost at Whittlesford station. Boxing in p.m.: at AA site, telling them that CO was trying to get them a gun. "Take cover" went at 3.30 p.m. One of the biggest battles of the war but nothing over us, though we heard bangs from Chesterford and Debden. Squadron Leader of the Canadian squadron landed, shot up with something in his eye, the first casualty in the sick bay. The Czechs have got 4 so far; Blackwood, their CO, had to bail out. To Red Lion Grantchester with Nigel – one pint of beer lasted two hours, talking! Journey home with no headlights. Went to a bad NAAFI show for an hour and then early to bed.

27th August 1940

Bumphkrieg in the morning and to see Thelma in the nursing home. Dog fight in the air above as I arrived. Back for lunch: most of the afternoon in the PMC's office, doing messing jobs. Long and trying "surgery" with men putting problems to me for which I can see no answer. Squash with Nigel. Ops room in the evening and watched the plot of a raid coming over here. Mild, very mild party with Nigel, Wedd, Boulton and Clarabutt. Bed at midnight.

28th August 1940

Talked to Harper about chaplain's work and explained various points. Boxing and bitting round camp till tea. Early supper and then to Q site (a decoy aerodrome) with Cooper to shoot game. No game in sight, so gave up at 8.45 p.m. Beer instead in two delightful pubs in Linton, especially the Bell. Home with German raiders overhead: saw and heard bombs fall on Cambridge at midnight.

29th August 1940

Into Cambridge in the morning, to fetch Mess food, in Mess Austin 7 (late Heath's): saw Thel. Wrote address in afternoon. Squash with Buckstone after tea. Busy clinic. Arranged with Boulton for removal of the kippers he has concealed in Oades' room to rot and smell to the discomfort of a deservedly unpopular older officer.

Took Ricks, a Czech airman, to play his squeeze box at Duxford B Post. The scene in the long canteen looked like a Dutch painting – the oil lamp, tin hats, and heavy shadows and then set faces looked more relaxed for once. The men loved it and made such a row the Germans must have heard! Alarm went at 9.45 p.m. and we came back. Bombs dropped on the K site at the time that Cooper and I had been there the other night.

30th August 1940

Flew with Boulton in a Tutor. He did some very unpleasant stalls and one spin and ended with a split-arse landing. He flies like a connoisseur, turning round after each acrobatic to savour it with you. Had an interview with Woody this morning, both of us wearing respirators! Laughing and choking so much I could hardly speak. To Q site in the afternoon: saw incendiary bombs and talked to the men. Flaps here after tea. Saw a Blenheim with a forward gun that fires to the rear, very cunning. Men to see me before supper. An Anson has run into the Met office!

31st August 1940

Air raid alarm began at 8.30 a.m. and continued off and on throughout the day. G1 bombed; no one hurt and no damage done, though there were ISO planes over there. Two men were sleeping in a tent when a bomb fell two feet away but no one was hurt. Many bombs filled up the craters that the others had made. Aberhart made a forced landing during the raid and was shot up and killed – a nice lad indeed. Coward got a canon shot through his leg. He was losing a lot of blood so he bailed out at 10,000 feet, and a delayed drop to 4000! Then as he floated down he made a tourniquet with his helmet: he has lost his leg. Frankie Brinsden bailed out near here but is unhurt. Czechs shot down seven planes. Went into Cambridge with Nigel at 5 p.m. to see Thel; dinner with Nigel at the Lamb.

1ˢᵗ September 1940

Usual services in morning. Saw Thel. Complication about Aberhart's funeral. Can't find his parents. Letters in the afternoon. 66 Squadron arrived. After tea went through Aberhart's things.

2ⁿᵈ September 1940

Arranging Aberhart's funeral. Into Cambridge in Mess car to see Thel. Afternoon bitting about station. Squash with Frankie Brinsden.

3ʳᵈ September 1940

Aberhart's funeral: rather a painful one. Afternoon went with Nigel to town in the car, giving Cooper a lift on the way – via North Weald, where we arrived just after bombs had fallen. Delayed action bomb in the road; aircraft on fire in the field; hangar blown up.

Dropped Cooper at Epping. Stayed at the Cumberland. To the Berkeley first of all for old fashioneds – Nigel maintains there are no others in London so good – and some highballs. Then to the Ivy; then to "Swinging the Gate" at the Ambassadors. Supper at an almost deserted Hungaria; private store of raw whiskey afterwards at the Cumberland. The raids seemed to be continuous.

Brian Lane (*centre*), one of No. 19 Squadron's most popular commanding officers. Lane was killed in 1942, age 25. CH 1366

4th September 1940

A little brittle this morning! But remarkably well, considering. Called at the "comforts" depot in Berkeley Square and loaded up with wireless sets, cigarettes and much else, and so reluctantly back, having sandwiches and a hair of the dog at the Cromwell in Stevenage. A really wonderful time. Nigel is the most pleasant companion, and it's good to have someone here at last to whom I can say what I like. I still feel dreadful about Peter and Bob. I suppose that helps to make me so restless.

5th September 1940

Cambridge in the morning on the way to G2. Saw Thelma and then out to G2 with wireless and other comforts. A lovely day and a happy time there. Got back here at 4.30 p.m. and heard, with a great shock, that Pinkham, the CO of 19, had been shot down and killed near Snodland at 10.15 a.m. This news has cast a gloom over us, for we liked him very much. He was young for his command but a grand man who evolved the new fighter tactics. He will find friends from his squadron waiting for him. Surgery this evening. Said goodbye to Harper who has been posted to Cosford. After supper talked to Smalley and Catter; later to them plus Howell and Boulton who was a little *exalté* after being in action for the first time.

6th September 1940

Woke up feeling very sad: partly Pinkham's death, partly the record of Bob's death in the casualty list, and partly an awful sense of the gap left by Peter.

Lane is the new CO of 19 Sq. This is well deserved. He ought to have had it immediately after Stevie was shot up. Every now and then one feels a bit bitter about Stevie.

Mr and Mrs Pinkham came to lunch. Boxing in the afternoon. Douglas Bader and his boys are operating from here. Saw him at tea. Heard that Peter King was killed a day or two ago. This is a sad knock. Peter once described him as the best type on the station. So he was. I saw him here last Sunday at lunch but hadn't a chance to say more than hello to his "There's the Padre." I shall miss him most awfully. It seems only a few days ago that he was in here asking should he get engaged to his nurse at Littleport R.A.F., poor little thing. Both the adjutants here, Smalley and Carter, thought well of him while he was acting adjutant of 66 Squadron. He did it so well. And that is high praise from two exacting critics. I wonder if he ever shot down the German that he said he would for Peter. Well, the two Peters are together again.

7th September 1940

Usual Sunday services. Last night Boulton was in fine fettle and bubbling over inside himself, so to speak. After a little prompting,

I found out that he'd shot down a HE 110 – his first combat and second operational flight. It fell down over the Goodwin Sands.

9th September 1940

Went round the distant DF stations with Howells. Had lunch at that very good pub at Stowmarket. Back here at 6.30 p.m. to hear that the wing had shot down 19 Germans. Everyone was safe except for Johnny Boulton. That came as a nasty blow and cold shock. He's missing.

10th September 1940

No news of Johnny Boulton. When I got back from Pinkham's funeral at St Andrew's, Well St., Kingsbury, there was still no news, so it seems he has been killed. Clarabutt, Wedd and I are in gloom, and so will Nigel be when he returns. I liked Boulton with his cuff shooting (he had the longest cuffs of anyone I've met); yesterday he was wearing his "ace" tough pullover, with silk neckerchief to match. He was the very picture of the most elegant pilot about to fight. He hadn't been here long; he came from a Flying Training School to show the Czechs how to fly Spits. He was much more intelligent than most of us here now. We had pleasant times; the evening at the Grantchester Red Lion, a good bathe on a sunny afternoon at Byron's Pool and many talks here over beer. Somehow he was a "very *parfit gentle* knight", too elegant for the R.A.F., you would have thought. He deprecated (he would use that word) the use of superlative language and he disliked slang, but he was the very best type. He was always very happy and gay. He was as near to an "exquisite" as it is possible to be in this kind of life and this year. Hunter and King, his air gunner of 264 Squadron, are posted missing, believed killed. O'Malley, the sensitive Winchester and the "House" lawyer and pilot of 264, has been killed in night ops. The waste is awful. All these – Boulton, Hunter, both the Kings, O'Malley – you would have wanted to make a decent world out of the bomb craters that will be left after this war.

11ᵗʰ September 1940

Sinclair came back today after his adventures on Monday. He bailed out and landed in Purley High Street! As he picked himself up, a young man walked across to help him. His only comment was "Fancy seeing you here, Gordon." News of Boulton: he crashed into Gordon and then into an ME and went down in flames.

15ᵗʰ September 1940

Douglas Bader has got the DSO, Eric Ball the DFC. This is as it should be and one wonders why Douglas wasn't given the DSO weeks ago. Sat in the hall after lunch and talked to his boys as they came in from a terrific air fight over London. The total score for the day is put at 185. Went on leave.

17ᵗʰ September 1940

Returned at 4 p.m. Pleasant surprise to find Nigel here for the night. Went with Smalley and Carter to Hildesham to fetch the ducks; drank beer with Mrs Smalley. Back here for supper and then to the Red Lion Grantchester for beer, rum and darts with Nigel and Derek Graham. Later Nigel and I drank beer in my room till the small hours, talking about the war, about Johnny Boulton, about God and bombs – a sermon he had heard at Christchurch Priory. It was a good evening and cheered me a lot. The Mess is usually so old these days. (When the pilots are away, the remaining officers are almost all veterans of World War One.)

18ᵗʰ September 1940

Up feeling as fresh as a daisy, or almost. Can it be that Nigel has a greater capacity for beer than I have? Anyway, as I walked over to the Mess I saw him flying away in his aeroplane to Christchurch. 9.30 a.m. watched the wing take off and form up overhead; then off to whip shit out of the Germans. In the afternoon went round G1's armoured car sites – 13 mile trip. Surgery and early to bed.

19th September 1940

An interrupted morning: alarms and chaps to be seen. Went to Cambridge to see Thel on her first time out. To the Q site. Tea here with Douglas Bader who described his adventures yesterday with the rear gunner of a Dornier who bailed out and got caught in the tail. It made the bomber aerobat. The other crew bailed out successfully. The Dornier did several loops; the man could not free himself, so, mercifully surely, Douglas, to use his word, "squirted" him.

The night barrage and bomb flashes over London have been visible this week. They are over here again with indiscriminate bombing; the cloud ceiling is very low. Douglas was saying how it makes him see red to find the Germans over London in the day time just plastering the civilians.

24th October 1940

Present position of station is that Bader and 242 Squadron are here: so are the Czechs; 19 Squadron is at G1. Whumps most nights, all so far misses, some of them near ones. Price, the padre under training, has been posted, Crankshaw replaces him. Dispute about Douglas's wing to be settled, probably in D's favour.

Have been seeing a lot of Derek Graham, of 5 RMU (Helicopters), who has been stuck here by bad weather and a helicopter U/S. He is an old Etonian and a nice one and prepared to talk seriously. I haven't persuaded him that there is a life after this one but from what he said I think it may appear as a more reasonable proposition. We have had one or two evenings at the Flint House, a pub which for some reason lends itself to theological discussion; we have talked further on return here.

Last night we went there again with Wick, another 5 RMU man, not a pilot, who is on a terribly secret affair. It was an interesting evening because I heard a bit about what we are doing in the way of research, and we had a long talk about "starlings", which was interesting. *(These were autogyros strapped to the backs of parachutists; Ian Little was experimenting with them.)*

This morning I was up early and prepared to fly with Derek to White Waltham in a Hornet to see Nigel. The weather didn't look too good, but we got reports and all was okay so we set off in the Hornet at about 9.45 a.m. It's a great honour to be allowed to fly in a 5 RMU Hornet: they let hardly anybody fly as a passenger. Derek had never flown it before so he made a circuit first, overshot but made a better landing the second time. So we took off and flew via Kings Langley, Beaconsfield to White Waltham. We arrived just in time to see Nigel step into the autogyro. However, we got down in time and had a short talk with him; then he went off, and we went to the Mess, had a beer and collected Derek's laundry, the real reason for the flight. We came back round by Marlow to see a bombed field – 100 craters in one field, a very pretty sight. Then we did an inadequate beat up of his aunt's house (near the stone crucifix we used to pass in peace time) and so low up the Thames to Maidenhead. It was looking lovely – the trees golden on the hills, the sun shone on the Thames and there were high clouds for a change. It was one of the most beautiful flights. Then we saw Nigel on his job and chased each other, and so returned to Duxford with a "but for the grace of God" landing. Derek remarked that I was intrepid to fly with him in the Hornet; but he wasn't as bad as that.

Group Captain "Boozey" Bowman in the Mess, very scented and affectionate. Pleasant to hear sergeants and officers in the RMU call each other by their Christian names.

Theme song of the period is "An Apple for the Teacher". There is a Canadian pilot who comes into the anteroom at 7.30 a.m. every morning and puts that record on without fail. Up to Dunkirk it was "Over the Rainbow" and "It's a Lovely Day Tomorrow".

On reflection, today's flight was one of the red letter ones – while we were over the North Road a Ju 88 was shot down near us at St Neots. Near Royston we argued whether it was Royston below and ahead. The camouflage is good. I said I wanted to see the Blue Plunge before I was sure; while we were arguing, there – staring out of the ground below us – was G1; there was nothing to be seen of Duxford till we were over it.

31st October 1940

Returned from 48 hours leave. On going I saw the wing take off and a Hurricane crash behind the DF station. Crankshaw was about so I didn't wait. It was a nasty sight to see the aircraft going in helplessly – sideways. Someone had hit his tail. The Czech pilot who got the DFC on Sunday was killed. When I got back here, there was a message for me to ring up Mrs Gillies. Bad news. He, Eric, has been picked up dead in the Channel and landed at Liverpool where the burial was. She is pregnant. One of the guards was accidentally shot by another this morning. That is the end of the tale of mortality.

Went to White Waltham on Tuesday and picked up Nigel; I got a room in the All Services Club – an odd place which had been a swimming pool. In Nigel's Mess we drank beer with another test pilot who has been doing this experimental ''night flying'' work; we also talked with the Belgians who were extraordinarily nice and not foreign like our Czechs, who are also nice. We dined at Skindles; next day up to town; lunch at the Ecu du France. Nigel knows how to live and eat. I slept in the afternoon at the Regent Palace after I called on Walter Wigglesworth who works for Intelligence in the bowels of the earth at the Air Ministry behind Church House. We three met at the Berkeley for old fashioneds and then to Quaglino's for some more and food; then to the United Universities for port and whiskey, and so to bed. It was queer in London at night. The streets are almost completely deserted and lit up by the eerie flashes from the flak. The tinkle of shrapnel falling on the roofs made us put on our tin hats. The walk was an experience that I shan't forget easily, more like being in Pompeii at an eruption than in the West End on an autumn evening.

Wallace 'Jock' Cunningham, Arthur 'Admiral' Blake and Francis Brinsden, all of No. 19 Squadron. CH 1459

All Souls Day 1940

Michael Lyne returned yesterday – with a stiff leg. We went to the Flint House and talked about 19 Squadron, the station, Peter and so on. This is not a happy day for there are too many souls to pray for and remember, and Michael brings back many remembrances of Peter.

News came today that Blake who has been missing since Tuesday has been killed – the details are not known yet. This is a blow to us all for he was one of the very best of the present pilots of 19 Squadron (the third or fourth generation since I came here) and one of the bravest. He was a Fleet Air Arm boy and we all liked him from the time of his arrival. One remembers him polishing his car endlessly at G1 and getting it "ship-shape". He would spend a long, long time on it, till it shone so much that there was no point in having it camouflaged. He was gentle with fine manners.

7th *November, 1940*

Returning from playing darts at dispersal with 242 Squadron this afternoon, saw a crashed "whirling spray", an autogyro, on the aerodrome. I assumed mentally and unkindly that it was Nigel! And it was! He came to tea and owned up to the crash. There is no room either for him or Ian Little in the Mess so they went to Cambridge. Joined them with Wicks later for sessions at the Bath and the Volunteer. Hitherto Ian has treated me as a well-to-do tenant farmer! Tonight he was naturally charming. Perhaps his shyness, like Derek's superciliousness, wears off. The Volunteer filled up with ghosts. Ghosts all the way back and Wicks added his quota from Debden with that of Hankey Hanson, the true "ace" from 111 Squadron.

Laurie Hart, the Canadian with the close-cropped hair and one of the friendliest, has been found dead. He was shot down on Tuesday. The Canadian boys haven't been here long but it does hurt losing them even as soon as this.

10th *November 1940*

Frankie Brinsden has been posted to the Polish Squadron at L. He has got his second stripe, so, alas, he had to go, to the real sorrow of us all. Perhaps he will teach the Poles how to squeal at squash!

Took Nigel in to Cambridge on Friday to see Thelma: we dined at "Toni's" and afterwards went to the Volunteer where there is always a welcome for this reverend.

Took the motorcycle to G2 today: lovely weather when I started off: no service there but given two rabbits instead. *(Motorcycle was an aged Triumph with a visible drip feed which I bought for £5 and used it to eke out the petrol coupons for my Hillman.)* Then came the rains, as they say in the films. I got back to Duxford, soaked to the skin. Took the 3 p.m. service in the church army hut, which is being used as the station church as it is more convenient and safer as it isn't on the operational side of the station. Made sandwiches afterwards with David Cox.

20ᵗʰ November 1940

Came back from seven days leave – perhaps the happiest time I've ever had. There was the joy of being with Thel and the new happiness of getting to know Robert. This is a war diary but that most important item must go in. Michael Lyne came over on Monday and we went to the University Library, looked in vain for a book by Craster's aunt on edible fungi. But we found a modern herbal which we thought would be useful. After tea we went to drink sherry with Francis Turner at Magdalene; drank it pretty smartly. Then with Thel to the Bath for dinner. Then back to the flat: Michael by this time was disinclined to return to Duxford, so I took off the top half of the divan and slept on that and he on the divan, in the front room. He went back next morning. Thel and I had a lovely drive to Newmarket on our last day. It seemed bitter that the leave was so short. Returned to find another chaplain u/t awaiting me, by name F.L. Trewella. I wonder about him.

21ˢᵗ November 1940

Went to Royston to see Harradene's baby. It looked as if it was dying. Managed to get him a sleeping out pass.

24ᵗʰ November 1940

Went to G2 on the AJS. It was a crisp day with a touch of frost and the best of days for the motorbike! Rather breathless and weather-beaten for the service. Home via Cambridge to see Thel; here for lunch to find Derek back.

After evening service went into Cambridge for dinner with Francis Turner in Magdalene. It was a lovely evening. It was good to see the candlelight in hall, but there are now no mitred napkins. The "Ram" was very gentle and charming. Salter was less aggressive. The Master was as charmingly stupid as ever. I arranged to bring officers for dinner from time to time. Lots of Irish whiskey and here by 11.00 p.m. Just said hello to "Happy Laughing Bassett" who fears he may be going to Canada. Involved in a long talk about God with two Canadian pilots till 3 a.m.

27th November 1940

This looks like being another exhausting week. The shaky hand is due to a bruise at squash. There seems to be no chance of going early to bed. Sunday night ended late on Monday morning; Monday night ended late on Tuesday. Derek talked and talked more seriously than usual and yesterday went on until about 2 a.m. We had a guest night for the AOC who is leaving the Group. He, AVM MacEwen, and Clouston and Frankie Brinsden were the guests. It went with a bang and ended, so I'm told, with a terrific melee in the hall after dinner. Both AVMs were made to dance on the table: Lane, for once, got surprisingly drunk – so drunk that he squeezed an orange over me. I replied in kind, and Cunningham emptied a pot of coffee over me. Was it surprising then that I took an early opportunity of pursuing the quieter occupation of talking to Craxton – of whom I've heard lots and lots but never met. He showed me how his dog, Fury, said its prayers, and then we talked till 1.00 a.m. or so about all manner of things: his photographic job, confirmation of himself and his wife. He insisted on seeing me home to bed which was quite unnecessary.

When I got to bed, I found that part of my denture was missing. I must have swallowed it. I made myself unpleasantly sick with a toothbrush, but the missing bit wasn't there, so the doctor sent me in this morning to Addenbrookes to be x-rayed; when I went to see Woody for leave he made some crude jokes about the danger of getting one's fingers bitten. Gave a lift to Kester, Lucky Leigh and Clouston who had sprained his finger. Kester passed himself off at the hospital as an army doctor and I got x-rayed without waiting. No sign on the first examination. On the second there was a trace, it was thought. The theatre sister exclaimed, "It might be a fly button" and without waiting pulled my trousers right down. But there is no trace so I assume that it has passed out in the natural course of events. No one in the hospital would take my plight and fears at all seriously; there was nothing but laughter in the Mess and where my snappers are alleged to be is the joke of the day.

1st December 1940

Thursday was a lovely day – no Friday: I went on the bike to Royston to see Mrs Harradene and the baby. Then I went to G2 where I found friendliness as ever and a number of odd jobs. Lunch with Thel in Cambridge. The afternoon was spent at K site where was another friendly time, spent in the hut, talking to the lads, drinking hot, sweet tea and being trounced at darts by a runner-up in the English championship. Someone said this week – and it is true – "Whatever your job in the service, you will always find someone else who can do it better." It was the day for a ride on a motorcycle – frosty, clear, high sky, with the sun, and cold enough to sting the face and nip the hands, but no worse. I enjoyed every moment of it and got back here about 5 p.m. feeling almost as if l had flown.

In the evening I took John Willy and Jeff (Jeffries of 310 Squadron – Czechs) to dine with the Mugger in Magdalene. I had given them strict orders about drinks before we met. These had not been entirely followed as I saw when I collected John at the Blue Boar. Jeffries at the Master's Lodge commented, as the Master opened a letter in the hall on leaving, "Not another bounced cheque, I hope." Fortunately, the point was missed. Sir Stephen Gazelee was there, and an old deadbeat who apparently had been CGS in the last war. The conversation turned on the battle on the August Sunday afternoon when we shot down 187 aircraft. Jeff who was in the forefront was asked if he had taken part; he looked vague and replied, "I don't remember." John was one of the few people by that time to shoot down an aircraft at night. He was asked, without foreknowledge, what fighting at night was like. He replied by indirect speech: "They say etc. …. I've been told." He made no reference to his own episode. When asked if he had shot down a ME at night he said, "No" and left them in ignorance that it was a Dornier. We sat in the Combination Room afterwards and drank Madeira. We looked through the oriel window at the wintry sky and the searchlights. Jeff asked, more politely than appears from this account, what contribution a Cambridge college and this kind of life made to the war effort. The Master stroked his moustache and then said, "We keep things going so that they will be ready for you when you come back. "If we come back ..." said Jeff, not really meaning at all to chill us all. A pleasant if not exciting evening which both. John and Jeff appeared to enjoy, probably unlike anything else they have experienced.

We got back at 11.00 p.m. to find 242 Squadron having its farewell party. More noise than anything else, but it got exciting when Tam and Stan started beating the drums in the hall, slowly at first and then faster and faster, till we should have burst with excitement if they hadn't stopped. Janoshek, the diabolical-looking Czech, was there, saying in French that there was always a little bit of Hell in him and that the Devil was always beside him. Certainly he looks like this. But Michael Wedd and I frightened him when we recited our *"Faites cette experience ... sans doute vous avez une maladie urinaire, tres, tres serieux."* He crumpled and went to bed. We had found how to exorcise him.

242 Squadron still here yesterday and today on account of the weather. Clouston has come from Leconfield with the nucleus of the NZ squadron he is forming. I am letting Trewella do most of the services today: alas, they don't seem very fond of him in the Mess, and I fear not without reason. He knows a little better than anybody else. He gives an impression of pompous wisdom and is full of clerical mannerisms. He needs his pants taking down: that would loosen him up mentally and spiritually. The others I have had have been such good types. But Trewella's war may be rather uncomfortable.

6th December 1940

Yesterday, Thursday, was a memorable day, and, as one would say, packed with incident. At 10.30 a.m. I left for Aston Down in the 310 Squadron Maggy with Chocolin as pilot. We had a fine flight there over Oxford and country I hadn't seen before from the air, which was thick with training planes, mostly Hudsons and Oxfords. We arrived at midday. I lunched early in the Mess with the chaplain – exceedingly nice. Then I set out for Dept. JJ of the Air Ministry; service transport to Minchinhampton and then bus to Tetbury and hired car to the palatial house outside. The department had left to form elsewhere, so back to Aston Down. The Maggy would only start after three quarters of an hour's winding. At 3 p.m. we set off, stopping or rather turning on the way to laugh at an Anson which had somehow force landed on a garden its own size, without damaging the hedges! How we laughed. A few minutes later, about 4 p.m., I realised that Chocolin was lost. I could see him in the mirror (I was in the forward seat). He spent most of the time looking at maps and in consequence we had too much of ups and downs for fun at 500 feet and went perilously close to some factory chimneys. He attempted to pass a map to me so that I could point out where we were. The map blew away in the slipstream. Then I identified St Albans. But we got lost again and at 4.15 p.m. force landed in a small park with trees on three sides. We had four shots before getting in (three touch downs and openings up – a nasty proceeding). Anyway, in we got. I walked across the park to a London bus; the passengers cheered; they thought we were brave fighter boys who had lost our way and come out of the jaws of Hell. The conductor showed me on the map where we were – three or four miles North West of Chelmsford.

We took off again, but the ground was heavy and we went straight for the hedge. I put my hands over my eyes as I thought we should go through it and cartwheel over the road. However, Chocolin pulled the stick back violently and up we came, but there was a "ping" noise. We had hit something, probably our wheels on a wire over the hedge. We scraped between trees and did a sharp turn back to see if our wheels were lying in the road and both of us laughed when we found they weren't. All the same, we knew it might be a difficult landing, so off we set for Debden. A few miles later on it was clear we hadn't enough petrol, so once more we tried to force land. First of all up-wind but the field sloped away too steeply and we should have gone over on our nose. We did a down-wind landing which is not pleasant. On the fourth time round, praying that the engine would not cut out, we touched down. Crump went the undercarriage, round went the plane, on its nose, smashing the prop, and out we stepped into the parish of Stebbing Green. I phoned Duxford and then came back to the plane to find that tea had been provided on a tray by a woman from the farm house opposite. We sat weak by the aircraft. We laughed and laughed as a reaction and in place of the relief and fear we felt. We had to stay there the night – W. Choppings, Collops Farm, Stebbing Green – (Mrs Choppings brought us the tea.)

It was a long, difficult evening, for the house was a teetotal one, and really we needed a bit more than hot sweet tea and godly conversation. There was a very pretty daughter and, after Chocolin and I had retired to an enormous double bed, he began to climb out, explaining that he would visit the daughter. A long and difficult argument followed in which I explained to him that this was not the English way. Reluctantly he accepted this, and, as he turned over to sleep, said, "I have before slept with many women, but with a priest – never." We laughed ourselves to sleep.

We were collected this morning and brought back to Debden. We got home at 1 p.m. for much leg-pulling and guffaws, but I'm told a near squeak was had by all. I knew this, and I remembered during our forced landings the people I had buried who sat in the front seat of a Maggy and how the engine came back on them. I was very uncomfortable while it was going on. However, the panicky fear did not exist: for one thing it was too late for fear, and for another, Chocolin handled the plane so ably and with terrific split-arse so that one felt confidence in him as a pilot, if not as a navigator.

10th December 1940

Second thoughts on the crash and discussion about it suggest that we had many very narrow squeaks. I remembered Peter's adage: "You never force land in a Maggy – you bail out."

Ian Little has returned from his tonsillectomy. Sanders to see me last night. He is panting to go in an air gunner: he is a nice lad, much too young, one would have thought, but with all the typical, simple English idealistic ideas.

12th December 1940

Went with Ian to the Flint House and then came back here talking till the very small hours about Spengler and Kant. It was perhaps the most interesting and lively conversation have had here, for he is an extraordinarily good conversationalist. Went with Smalley to the University Library to do researches into heraldry about the station coat of arms. Gave Nigel (who came this morning) and Ian a lift in and out. A pleasant surprise in the Mess for tea: Rupert Leigh and Bob Oxspring have arrived.

Questions about Nicholson, the first VC of Fighter Command. The feeling in the Mess is that surely he must have been line-shooting in his account of his hands being on fire or else that the papers put more into his mouth than he said. But this evening one of Nicholson's airmen came to see me. He told me that he saw him afterwards, or rather saw his flying kit, and that the skin of Nicholson's hand had adhered completely to the rip cord of his parachute and had come off.

16th December 1940

Lucky Leigh down on Friday with Bob Oxspring and we had something of a reunion. He told me that, when the report of our crash in the Maggy had been passed to him at Group, he had noted: "I cannot believe this: this Padre would not force land so far away from a public house."

Went with Ian in his car with the loose front seat after luncheon on Sunday to the DF station at Barton Bendish: an amusing ride as the driver's seat slips backwards and forwards, causing amusement to all save the driver. Did my stuff at Barton Bendish and went on to the Rose and Crown at Wisbech, getting there about 5.30 p.m. – a good dinner with better wine. The claret was good and the claret

An unfortunately anonymous photograph of Rupert 'Lucky' Leigh, another of Guy's close friends, and Commanding Officer of No. 66 Squadron. HU 59063

excellent. The waiter was uneasy at serving us with brandy. But we both twitched our faces and our shoulders jumped during the evening so that he understood we were war-worn heroes. At one stage he said, "This is a very expensive wine, sir." Ian replied, "Good. I only drink expensive wine." We talked again far into the small hours, a lot about Ian's philosophy: it's hard to refute, for, when it's not almost more dogmatic than any Christian dogma, it's woolly. However, it was amusing for he can talk, is always interesting and puts his points well. I like the sound of his friends, particularly the one who is in Greece. Ian looks a babe, but he is more mature than you might think at first meeting. Much talk about how to build bungalows. We started back at 10.45 a.m. next morning through deserted fen country which has always given me the creeps. More arguments on the way back. Have got to know Ian quickly now that his self-consciousness has gone.

Returned by 1 p.m. to find Nigel back. Walked into trouble. Woody sent for me and said, "Either that chaplain Trewella leaves the station or I do. What will you do?" Woody, choking with passion, told me that Trewella had come up to him in the anteroom; he had ignored the rows of medals, the brevet and the four rings and had asked him, "Have you been long in the service? How long have you been on the station?" The result must have been one of the great silences of history. I telephoned QJ at once. Trewella goes this evening; he is a bloody nuisance. Elphic, a new chaplain u/t, booked to come tomorrow. Felt better for a game of squash with Vokes: it's whipped the brandy and claret out of me. Yesterday was very enjoyable and the eeriness of that fen country strikes me more than it ever used to.

Played bridge – without commotions – with Applee, an army officer and Ian. I thought I did very well but no one else did.

Reflections on the various conversations with Ian suggest that he is blessed with great candour which perhaps balances his introspectiveness. This is all a bloody business. I try to keep this diary factual and make it merely a record. It's as well. I feel I am losing the faculty for constructive, analytical thinking about myself. All one's work is giving out; there's little chance for anything to come in in return. I don't analyse my own reactions to events critically enough. It's a pity; it would help if I could. One goes from experience to experience, hoping that the total will survive into peace if one lives to see it. So, too, one makes friends and makes them faster with the more intelligent and prays that this too may survive. I pray that I may contrive to persuade the honest doubter about Christianity. I wonder sometimes how far the pace with which one gets to know people in these days of a short future and few reservations make it harder to convince them. It didn't with Peter and Bob. But I see now the mistake of not presenting Christianity as essentially a matter for reasoning faith.

18th December 1940

Had dinner last night at the Bath with Thel, Nigel and Ian. It was a terrific evening with laughter on the most lavish scale. Looking back the main impression is one of larking from 8 p.m. to 1.45 a.m. Ian was in particularly fine form and reduced me to baffled silence several times. We left after ten and drove back, stopping once outside Trumpington to pee and chase Ian about a quarter of a mile down the road, although why I can't remember. The fog was bad and it took us an hour to get back. A little beer here and a modest de-trousering of Ian who had become quite intolerable. I've never met anyone with such a gift for conversation, usually original, always amusing, and full of repartee. This is one of the happiest evenings I have had for a long time. Nigel is still here. He always is when he says he must leave "first thing".

Took Elphic round and about the station this afternoon and morning – Sick Bay at Thriplow, GI and so on. He is someone you can take about.

Ian has put up a "black" on his birthday. He developed a film in the bathroom last night. Now the bath is a muddy colour and nothing will move the stain. Ian's first film home-developed looks like being expensive. Great stir in the Mess among the older officers. There is resentment about Ian and Nigel: "Why aren't these young chaps flying on operations? Why are they here in safe jobs?" Neither of them can reply for themselves for the work is very secret, any more can those of us who know what they are doing. Their tenure on life is no more secure than that of any operational pilots; Ian perhaps has the more perilous job. Played squash with him this evening and bathed in the stained water without ill effects.

I get tired of the sterile mood induced by war. Circumstances and emotions stimulate one to some form of expression, and then nothing happens. I want to write but I can't: it comes out drab stuff. I would like to write some poetry but when the time comes, as with prose, ended with nothing more than a mere record. The mind is not able to take a free rein. Yet half the time I am under emotional strains that I've never experienced before.

It's the same with reading. With verse I like the well-tried ones that I know. I haven't the energy to read new ones unless they are bad. So also with prayer. There is so much to say, so much of which I want to make conscious expression – Thelma, Robert, one's friends, the future of the war, the station and so on – yet I can't get further than a series of recollections, a consciousness of God and a general awareness of him. There is much experience but nothing specific.

I'm sure that half the secret of such duty as I attempt to do is to keep myself ready to learn – not so much from facts, as from other people's characters. Living in mess makes for a variety that I haven't experienced before. And see what happens here: one night you have an airman like Sanders with his simple and honest intentions of duty. The next night it may be J. Russell Budd for once trying to see the wood for the trees and being simple behind his facade of bombosity; or again there is the quick receptiveness of Nigel; or the gentle obtuseness of Derek who tends to put a wrong interpretation on common experience; or the clear-cut, inexhaustible enthusiasms of Ian for abstract thought and argument. At the other extreme is Carter with his simple religion and the smell of the fires of Smithfield still in his nostrils. You become the keeper of their consciences. There is so much to remember, so much to forget.

Sometimes, particularly with the older men, the privilege of confidence is a burden, a happy one in one sense, but still a burden. Looking back – I'm thinking now of the younger ones – I wonder whether I have been too candid. Perhaps it is my job to see all, hear all and say nowt. I don't think so. I get candid now with particular people: it's a relief not so much to open one's grief, for the grief can't be put down in words, but to realise that we are being open.

Whatever may come now, I feel I have lived and this doesn't apply by any means to service life. I'm thinking of Thelma and what she is to me. I told Nigel once that I was a Christian pagan. It's a meaningless phrase and slovenly, but in the context I meant that I do feel a sense of fulfilment, which is not the same as achievement – of that I can't judge.

20ᵗʰ December 1940

I had hoped to go to bed early. The last few or many evenings have been late ones on account of metaphysical discussions with Ian and Nigel. I went to the Corporal's Dance. Woody wanted me to go with him to the Sergeants Mess. I went. He drank enormously. I drank the polite minimum. Had too long talks with Sergeant Pilots, one of whom I thought was cold sober till he fell off his stool. Woody passed the point of no return in drinking. Kester, the station warrant officer who was a Cambridge solicitor in another life, and I got him to his shooting brake.

I drove him to his quarters in Duxford village where he lived, he being propped up in the seat next me. We passed the sentries without incident as the car was flying his pennant and I wasn't stopped. I opened the window and said, "Station Commander" and it sufficed. We put Woody to bed but not finally to bed – we undressed him enough to make him think that, when he woke up, he had been able to see to himself, and left him. We left his car at his house and walked back.

Tradition coped with the situation next day. When I came into the anteroom before dinner, I made a little bow to him. He was in his usual place, his feet on the kerb of the hearth. His poached egg eyes, exaggerated by his monocle, were more blood-shot than usual; but he was himself – he was in control. He was the station commander. He looked up and with the slightest of slight nuances and a quick look, he got the first word in: "You all right after last night?" It might have been a dangerous opening, but by this time I had learned my piece. "Splendid, sir. Will you have a gin?" He did. It was a good way of conveying to me that he realised what had happened and was grateful.

I meant to go to bed at 9.30 p.m. but Ian turned up with Madeira, and once more he demonstrated the real art of conversation, now on the way to being lost.

Cox, the Assistant Chaplain-in-Chief, paid a short visit. Lunched at Corpus with Sir Will Spens and R.A.F. nobs to discuss the problem of the influx of airmen into Cambridge at night.

21st December 1940

I intended to go to the WAAF Christmas dance but l have a bad catarrh. The fug in the hut, owing to the black-out, was so awful that I left after a few minutes.

Went on the bike to Cambridge this morning. It's so cold and icy that my head ached, and that got rid of the catarrh – frozen away, I suppose. Found Thelma rather depressed because she is so tired with the preparations for moving. Had a wonderfully happy time as we always do ... Gave Ian a copy of A.E. Taylor's "Faith of a Moralist" for the good of his mind. This morning he thanked me and added

"I've not read it all yet." Suppose you had to choose one member of the present Mess to exist with you on a desert island, would it be Nigel or Ian? I would refuse to go unless both came.

It's difficult to convince myself that a year ago as a journalist I could write 2000 coherent words at short notice on almost any subject for the public to read. There are lots of things to write about but my mind is like a pending tray with the unsorted papers that remain till they can be destroyed. One snatches at happiness so hard that I want to keep the records stabilised in my mind. And that is impossible. Here is an unsorted list of conversational topics with Ian – cameras, bookmakers, new ways for defeating economic slumps, aircraft, the more intellectual pilots and the way they are treated by the more stupid of their fellow officers, philosophy and sex. This last is not so interesting because there is nothing new under the sun. But all the other subjects remain unfinished. I want to hear more about the betting system. I add to the list – family fortunes, family cellars, the future of wine and curious relations.

I came to my room at 8 p.m. this evening to read. I can't settle. I wrote duty letters. Read two poems by Hardy which I didn't understand; I ate my last jujubes; I have written this; I shall go to bed.

22ⁿᵈ December 1940

Celebrated communion and let Elphic go to the AA sites. I went with Ian to the mass inhumation sites to watch Wicks dispose of 500 incendiaries and some pyrotechnic oddities. These last shot red stars with great violence. They shot away from us, but there was no reason why they didn't shoot at us. The bombs made a lovely, long, fierce blaze. We hopped about taking photos. Some of the bombs proved to be explosive. This made it more exciting. It was extremely cold and even the lecherous Warrant Officer Greg looked frozen. It was a very happy Sunday morning and reminded me of peace time Sundays when we did small and exciting things instead of going to church.

To G2 for Christmas arrangements. Long hot bath. Dinner in Cambridge with Thel and Ian who was in his "enchanted mood" as

Thel describes it. We drank at the Panton Street Arms, thence to the University Arms where Ian made the porter telephone the Bath for a table, but in the end we dined at Tom's with Ian as host. We came back and drank Madeira here, Ian and I agreed that when the war was over we should have to shoot a lot of older officers. So ended a very happy Sunday.

25th December 1940

Queer and sad Christmas Day. I only remember one other away from home and that was when I was a curate in Fitzroy Street. Going to celebrate communion in the Church Army hut at 7 a.m., a radio was playing "Home Sweet Home". It hit me. The car would not start, so after breakfast I went on the bike to the AA post and to G2. It was bitterly cold. Good services at both places. Saw Thelma on the way back and reached the Mess for the tail end of the Sergeants' party. To the Airmen's Mess to serve dinner. I learned a new bit of English idiom: "Have you had any turkey?" "Yes, thank you. I've had my dinner." (But he had not had his pudding). Then I went to the sick bay, the dispersed sick bay, G1 and the K site. The car was now working, thank heaven. Tea and after that squash with Bill Smith of AFDU. To bed, dog-tired, at 9.30 p.m. Before going to sleep I read a chapter on 'The Decomposition of Cadavers in Water'.

All the day the Czechs had a Christmas tree with candles lit on it. Round the candles were the names of their dead. I was glad they counted Johnny Boulton among them. It has been a curious day.

27th December 1940

Lunch and tea with Thelma. Squash with Wedd who is about to fulfil his ambition of becoming an operational pilot. Ian and I talked till 1 a.m.

28*th* December 1940

Met Thelma in Cambridge. Met Ian at the Volunteer and returned for the WAAF cocktail party. It was dull but we did our best to make it expensive. AVM MacEwen danced the Highland fling. Wing Commander Vass, who is nearly seven foot tall and built to measure, kept begging me to call him Tiny: "Don't call me, 'Sir'."

29*th* December 1940

Impressive thoughts as to the futility of looking forward to anticipated pleasures.

31*st* December 1940

Ian and I had dinner at the Bath. He had a simple, solid meal, two mixed grills served in succession. Then we went to the cottage at Linton. We sat up late talking and it ended with a bridge lesson which I failed to understand, to his impatient contempt. (The house was empty; Thel was moving to it in a day or two.) We dossed down on the floor and slept. Feel frail this morning.

Saw combat film – grim and exciting and it manages to convey something of what one imagines a dog fight is like and of waiting to be dived on. New Year's Eve party in the Sergeants Mess. I only stayed an hour. I could not bear it any longer. There is nothing to sing about this year. I crept back here to sleep and to try not to think about the thunder and lightning which is threatened to come upon us very soon. I hadn't the heart to sing Auld Lang Syne in the bloody world as it now is. This is no time for "old acquaintance". Who'll be left to remember? If it is remembered next year, how much of it without bitterness and sadness, how much of it will be remembrance of times lost, of things left unsaid and unshared? I can't sing when we are on the edge of an abyss once again and about to be robbed of comrades and friends as we were last summer. The summer was one of brilliant sunshine, heat, shimmering landscape; I remember walking to the Mess every day with the impression that the sky was black and heavy as lead.

Ian goes to Mildenhall tomorrow and I hope I go on leave. It looks like being the end of a chapter. It's unlikely that Ian will be here again for so long at a time. We have spent almost every free night in talk. I have felt once again that I have got friends, with Nigel and Ian, though Nigel has virtually left here and is at Wick. As touching the service, I feel established again, though both Nigel and Ian are very different from Peter.

All of this last is pleasant to write, pleasant and happy to think about. There is Thelma and the blessed Robert with his continual and exuberant laughter. There is this most precious substance between me and what may come to us in the New Year.

I don't doubt for a moment that we shall win the war. But l can't doubt that we shall suffer and that gay and good people will go down.

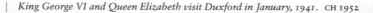

| *King George VI and Queen Elizabeth visit Duxford in January, 1941.* CH 1952

1941

5th January 1941

Returned from leave feeling desperately homesick. This is a measure of the happiness and enjoyment we had. Much of the leave was spent in trying to make the cottage warmer. I miss Robert. I am very happy about him. To return here and enter the anteroom is like stepping from a warm bath into ice cold water. Budd's vulgar obtuseness, greasy Applee, the loud-voiced Woody. I wish I could live this sort of life without making friends and only make acquaintances. I'm not made that way, so I must go on gaining and losing.

11th January 1941

There is a cloak of dullness over Duxford. There are no excitements. There are no friends in the Mess. I have been developing films and prints with Randall, the dentist.

16th January 1941

Spent yesterday afternoon in the dismal task of arranging Chappell's funeral. I saw his wife yesterday. They were married in July, 1940. Went to a dance at the K site in the evening. It was freezing hard, snow on the ground and a moon which made everything as light as daytime. The King and Queen came to lunch today. He gave out "gongs" in the hangar after lunch but not before there had been a row. The gongs had not come. It was suggested to HM that he should merely shake the pilots by the hand. He wasn't having this.

Regardless of discipline and everything else, he walked up and down the anteroom and later in the corridor outside telling Woody and the AOC very loudly that, unless the gongs came, he was going away (after explaining to the pilots why he couldn't present them). There was some demurring about this. There were red and excited faces and loud voices. The last words I heard from HM were these, icy cold and with his stammer: "Very well. Get me the Air Ministry on the secret line and I'll talk myself." The gongs came.

The Queen, as they say, looked a picture. She really did. No bullshit. She may have a figure like a dumpling well-camouflaged but the result is one of great charm and grace. She flashed her smile around and won all hearts. Applee managed to play shuv ha'penny with her, but we didn't allow him to keep the coins.

The anti-climax came when HM went off to Debden. He was preceded by one of our cars carrying the autographed photo of the sovereign which hangs or should hang in every R.A.F. mess. Both Debden and Duxford have lost theirs: we borrowed the Bassingbourn photo.

20th January 1941

MacKnight and Latta of 242 are missing. They have been shot down over the Pas de Calais. There is a chance that they may have been rescued in the sea but this is not the weather for picking pilots out of the drink, nor is it suitable for pilots waiting in the drink to be rescued. MacKnight was short and wiry and tough. If anyone had asked me what a typical pilot of fighter command was like, I could not have done better than to introduce MacK. It's snowing again and bitterly cold. I had to cancel the Sunday service at the sites; instead I went round the perimeter on foot to the gun sites and PAC sites distributing woollens from the comforts store. Played shuv ha'penny with Craster and Nigel for most of last evening.

Eric Ball (left) 'Willie' McKnight (right) and the irrepressible Douglas Bader (centre). McKnight was killed in January 1941. CH 1412

23rd January 1941

Have been in the doldrums for days. Invasion is on the cards again. The spring seems to contain little but a renewal of old horrors and some worse ones in store. Went to Linton for lunch with Thel, en route for the Q site.

27th January 1941

Thelma, Nigel, Ian and I dined at the Whittlesford Red Lion and then returned to the Cottage for talk. We talked about books; I was glad that we were able to produce from our shelves all the books mentioned.

Ian has been taken ill and rushed to hospital.

Called at Pembroke College to see Fr. Wilfred Knox but he was out. There is a great weight of heaviness hanging over the Mess. Owing to the weather there have been few raids during the past week. But everyone is apprehensive about what lies in store for us in the spring.

29th January 1941

Lovely afternoon at home. Left sadly at 9.30 p.m.

3rd February 1941

Rumoured that gas will be used in the spring. Our gas defences are being overhauled. Went through the gas chamber this morning with a respirator and afterwards without it. The latter trip was extremely unpleasant. Thomas, the new signals officer, a Yorkshireman, tells me that the Yorkshire fishermen towed rescued German pilots home by their feet and with their heads under the water. I can believe this.

9th February 1941

Came to Linton on the start of leave. Before I left, we had a sherry party in the Mess. Thel came, and so did Ian, now free from hospital, and Nigel. We drove home. Forgetting that the snow and the thaw would affect water levels, I took the short cut through the ford. The car stuck. We got cold and wet trying to push it out. We left it till morning, and Nigel and Ian dossed down in the dining room. We got the milkman to tow the car out in the morning and it started at once.

I set off for Yorkshire by car as the weather was too bad for flying. I dropped Ian at Goole station. What a grim place it is! Then I came alone over the Wolds to Bridlington. There are no walks on the beach. There are soldiers everywhere, and some signs of bomb damage. The town is drear and desolate. It's sad to be home in grey times. There is not much hope in evidence. It's useless to make plans for the future. Even so, it is Yorkshire and it is home. It is good to hear the broad accent and to see the ugly Methodist chapels.

15th February 1941

Returned to find excitement. A Dornier with its lights on landed last night on the flare path at Debden. It followed one of our bombers in. The German pilot walked to the watch office and asked the way (where to?) with a strong accent. He didn't wait for a reply but took off again. He repeated this performance at Newmarket and at Feltwell. On all occasions the duty pilot in the office was flabbergasted and the German ran off into the darkness before he could be shot. I am told that, if he comes here, he will be compelled to stay. I was outside the cottage yesterday evening watching a plane with its lights on going into Debden. Thelma remarked that it sounded like a German. And so it was.

On the last afternoon of leave I drove with Thelma round the countryside. The woods near the Four Went Ways were full of aconites. We stayed in for the evening and had a colossal steak. I am heavier than ever Thelma imagines at coming away. Robert is enchanting. He is a darling son.

On leave, mother and I went to Scarborough; we lunched and shopped, as in happier times. I am sad at leaving father and mother at home. Bridlington is not a safe place. Father gets old and feeble. Mother is wonderfully cheerful and strong. They think they would rather remain in what comfort they have and be near to Dr Chapman than to move.

16th February 1941

A German tried to land at Bassingbourn's satellite last night. He is still with us.

17th February 1941

Four German Para troops landed near Waterbeach. They have all been rounded up. One was soon arrested for he was seen wearing natty pin stripes and fawncoloured spats. These seemed to be out of place at night in the Fens.

Scrambled eggs, bread and jam and a long, huge tea at G1. The stove was almost red hot all the way up. I was asked by 19 Squadron to prevent Haines from marrying his latest – a half-Italian female.

19th February 1941

Tea at home yesterday. A Dornier cruised over us at 500 feet towards Debden.

In the evening I went with Tommy Tucker, Ian and Nigel to the Flint House where we talked wistfully about food and how to cook it.

20th February 1941

Michael Lyne has returned for duty with 19 Squadron and without a stiff leg. Leonard Haines has been posted to Halton in an attempt to save him from marriage.

Lunch with Thel. Robert used his playpen for the first time and uttered cries of ecstatic delight.

21st February 1941

Thelma, Nigel, Ian and I dined at the Bath – two mixed grills for Ian. We returned to Linton and talked, Robert intervening, till 12.30 a.m. It was a happy evening. If you stop to think or let undisciplined thoughts creep in as to what may be coming, things are not so happy. God bless all. I'm sleepy. God bless Thelma and Robert especially.

24th February 1941

Had a vivid dream about Bob Emmett last night. Thel and I and Robert were enjoying a picnic. The truth came when I woke up. The dream hung about all day and would not disperse.

Went to London by train. Walked about the City and the West End, looking at the damage. I saw the ghastly crater where Bank Underground station used to be, with the bridge over it. Everything looked ghastly and sad. Dinner at the United Universities Club in honour of Samuel Pepys, with Walter Wigglesworth, Tony Bull, Tony Butler, John Ellis (all contemporaries at Magdalene) and the secretary of the Admiralty who is Pepys' successor. I didn't enjoy the event and felt distrait. Walter is better alone anywhere, anyway. Stayed at the Regent Palace and had breakfast in the restaurant. This was a mistake. You see the kind of people who stay in London these days.

25*th* February 1941

This silly idea for training on an operational station has had serious results. We had 12 bombs on the flare path this evening. No one has been killed but there has been a good deal of damage. One stick interrupted a game of chess which Ian and I were playing. People playing bridge went under the table very quickly. We started playing again. The second stick began to fall. The veterans of the last war hurried from the Mess with excuses of duty. Ian and I decided we would go on playing, whatever happened, just to show. When the veterans returned, having changed their pants, they found us still concentrating on our game, or so it looked.

26*th* February 1941

I was wrong. Two Czechs were killed last night.

3*rd* March 1941

Ah God, to see the bombers stir
Across the moon at Grantchester.

A Cierva autogyro, or 'whirling spray' to Guy. These machines were used – with much discretion – to help calibrate radar, and were flown by his great friends, Nigel Browne and Ian Little. CH 1426

Returned from the Red Lion, Grantchester with Nigel. The beer was nasty. The landlady sent her love to Thelma and Robert, whom she wants to see. Ian has gone to Plymouth; Derek has returned looking very ill and shaken after his crash. Spent the afternoon at WA1. The Mess here in the doldrums, all waiting apprehensively to find out whether, now that the station has been made a Group-Captain post, Woody (who is a Wing Commander) will remain.

Very happy afternoon with Thel and Robert.

4th March 1941

Flew with Nigel in the autogyro – curious experience. It shudders and wobbles before it takes off and then jumps up. We flew to Linton and beat up Thelma and Robert. Nearly got written off by a Gladiator which didn't see us when it was landing; it landed under us when we were 50 feet up.

5th March 1941

———

Thel's evening out: supper at the bath with Nigel. Back to Linton for a garrulous and giggly time; back here 2.30 a.m.

7th March 1941

———

Tea in Cambridge with Thel and Nigel.

9th March 1941

———

Woody is going, owing to Saul (the new AOC at Group) disliking him, and owing also to admin slackness for which Woody is held responsible. The problem is: how will Woody get cleared of debts? He has gone to see Leigh Mallory *(the old AOC, then AOC of a southern Group)*. The new CO is Tiny Vass who is now a Group Captain. The Mess reminds me of something I read about the death of the French King at Versailles: "as soon as it was perceived that there was no hope for His Majesty, the palace was filled with the sound of thunder; the noise was of the courtiers running across rooms and passages to greet the Dauphin, the new King."

Thel came to the concert in the hangar this evening – Maurice Cole and May Harrison. A very happy evening.

10th March 1941

———

Went to WA1 [formerly G1] with Craster and Evans (engineering officer); we were beaten up by Sergeant Charnock who came over B Flight dispersal in his Spit at about 50 feet.

Woody returned from his visit to Leigh Mallory: he is much more cheerful, particularly as he has come back with the OBE which he gracefully announced was for "Other Buggers' Efforts" (a nasty smackdown for Saul). Budd remarked yesterday that, if Woody must go, it was better to have a devil you know than one you don't.

Told Woody how sorry I was he was going: both embarrassed and simultaneously rang the bell for the waiter for drinks.

13th March 1941

"Ace" Pace came. He has six weeks sick leave, after severe facial burns and wants to spend them on the station. I am afraid his face looked dreadful; it calls for an act of will to look at him when you talk to him. Applee and I have talked to Woody, for Ace's face is the worst thing for the pilots' morale – visible effects on them already. We have arranged for him to spend his leave in Shelford, but without his being aware, I hope, of the reason. He is sensitive about having his photo taken; so I took it for his new identity card.

Played squash with Rod Bodie, the new Flight Lieutenant of 310 Squadron. He is a good foil for Dizzy Davis, the other Flight Lieutenant. Rod was here with 66 when I first came and has been with them all the time they were in the south. He gave me a photo of Peter King and Gillies (I gave the latter to his wife.)

16th March 1941

Flew yesterday in a Boston, now called the Havoc. It was on an endurance test and we flew for two hours round the sector – Cambridge, Peterborough, March, Thetford. I sat in the bomber's seat under which is the undercarriage. It is a terrifying experience taking off for the wheel bounces under you and vibrates as if it were about to fall off. It's a tricycle undercart, so lands nose down very fast. The sensation was that of going straight into the deck. Flew over all the country I covered with Peter last year before the war really started. There were many landmarks. We could see fog over the Norfolk coast going up like a solid wall to 6000 feet. We flew at 5000 feet just under the cloud.

Thomas Gilbert 'Ace' Pace was, to Guy, an 'old school' fighter pilot. Tragically, he was badly wounded in early 1941 and was later killed in December of the same year.

3rd April 1941

Woody has gone; a grand party to see him off. Money was found to pay his mess bills. Pete Gordon got drunk and hit me while the MO and I were putting him tidily to bed. So without thinking I knocked him down with one blow and was very surprised indeed. Then we gave him a cold bath and left him. He wrecked Wing Commander Allen's room, but who cares? He flew away at dawn.

Took Rod home to see Thel. Went to Balsham and Rod told his incredible story about the Salvation Army and how he got into the R.A.F.. Had his 21st birthday party last night and is suffering from one hand strained and the other bitten this morning. At first sight he gives the impression of a horrid raw toughness; but behind it is a queer imaginative sense of humour. He makes life more enjoyable. All my friends are on the station now; Ian and Nigel have returned and there is a wide company of close acquaintances. Woody is missed; we shall like Vass better when we have broken him to the peculiar ways of Duxford. Smalley said today, "The best thing about new brooms is that in sweeping clean they soon break their handles."

8th April 1941

Very fed up and sour. Vass is fussing and rubbing everyone up the wrong way. He inspected my PSI accounts and was critical of the way they are kept. They are all in order but not kept as in the peace time service. He was surprised when I said I would gladly give them up at once and that he would need a clerk: I hadn't the time and it wasn't my job anyway. I have now been supplied with a clerk, Stevens.

Rod and I arranged to go to London this evening; everything packed in the panic bags, but all leave stopped; there is a flap; expecting a blitz and there are to be night patrols.

Thel and I had a modest party the other night at the Grantchester Red Lion for "lngha", Michael, Roger and Rod. Thel talked later about how hard it is when you get to like operational pilots like Rod.

9th April 1941

Instead of spending last night at the Berkeley with Rod, went to WA1 to spend it with 19 Squadron. Special patrols; stayed up there for two or three hours; Dizzy, Rod, Burda, Jeff and some other Czechs, Chiefy Lane and others of 19 Squadron. It was a well-remembered evening. The very alternating current in the Nissen hut; the red-hot stove; pilots in various stages of sleep and undress or full flying kit; games of shuv ha'penny or talk of comments on the pin-up girls interrupted by phone calls as Ops sent off patrols after "bandits". I left at 10.30 p.m. just as Jeff shot down a Heinkel. One of those evenings when the door opens, out goes a pilot for a patrol and you don't know whether he will come back to pick up the conversation where he left it off or whether you will never see him again. It's horrid and grim; it would be easier if one didn't like them and get fond of them. The gayest and most effervescent is the Elizabethan spirit of Dizzy swearing through his terrible stammer and always happy. In this century he has a Hurricane and a pilot's ticket; in another century he would have been the master of a frigate sailing under letters of marque.

We are getting near the season when there will be some last good nights and goodbyes to be said.

Whenever I motor, I sing the hymn "Think O Lord in mercy" and turn to Peter and Bob in thought. The obscurity of their deaths may be a mercy for us. Sometimes when I'm playing squash I suddenly find myself wrenched into remembering the hundreds of games Bob and I had at Weybridge in the deserted squash court; or it always seemed unused; but I suppose other people played at other times. We came to regard it as our own. It wasn't so happy driving home from Weybridge when the war started and the barrage balloons were flying, for Bob knew that his call would come any day.

Maunday Thursday, 1941

The depression is hard to shake off. There is bad news from Libya and the Balkans; and there is the ever-present fear of what may come to us here. Today has been warm, unclouded and full of sunshine. But it seemed overcast in reality, and not even the Swastika which Dizzy traced over the Mess in a vapour trail for all East Anglia to see (it caused panic) cheered us up. Squash yesterday with Peel, the horse-faced bomber pilot from AFDU. He beat me. This evening beat Rod; we both played badly. I read his log book as we got dressed. There is one characteristic entry: "Canon shell hit aircraft; aileron fell off; bullet wound in leg." The next entry for the following day is another combat report.

Killick (a chaplain) here to see Harkus, the O.D. padre now posted here.

15th April 1941

Another evening during night patrols at WA1. Phone blasting all the time and then the weather closed in and all was packed up. Sunday was Easter Day – very happy. Good services. Went for a long walk with Rod on the tarmac to get cool. Standing by for another night of patrols after a full day of operations at Kirton in Lindsey. Both 19

Squadron and 310 Squadron are being worked much too hard during these moonlit nights. Am seeing as much as I can of Rod. Who knows?

Went with Thel to see the Budds last night. Mrs Budd told me that a Pilot Officer was reading the lesson at evensong in a church in Wales; he read "'And Moses said – and Moses said' and if this damned book would stay still, I'd tell you what he did say."

17th April 1941

Have been trying to go home all this week to see Thel. Arrangements have always been broken – night flying and patrols. Awful raid on London last night. Rod described it to me. He was patrolling there for two hours but saw no Germans; what he saw below made him so angry that he felt he would have rammed a German if he had seen one.

25th April 1941

Duke of Kent came here on Tuesday to inspect welfare arrangements. I trotted him around with Vass for three hours. He continually puts his handkerchief to his nose as though there were scent on it; maybe there is. Insisted on seeing me alone in my office and told me to phone him at Buckingham Palace if there was any difficulty I couldn't overcome; he added that he could talk to his brother about it, too. Inspected the airmen's mess, and I pointed out our wonderful soup cauldrons, all steam-heated, and invited him to have a taste. I saw the Sergeant cook purple with excitement and went over to find out what was wrong: it wasn't soup, it was tea. I explained to the Duke before he drank it. Took him to WA1 to see 16 Squadron; stopped by angry sentry who demanded passes and laughed when I said, "Duke of Kent and Group Captain". Finally the party was let through on my pass after some embarrassing back-chat about leg-pulls from the sentry.

Woody returned on Tuesday to have his fourth ring sewn on. Then he went off to command at Tangmere. So his story had a happy ending: he has now got the most important fighter station in England. Saul

'Rod' Bodie and his fiancé, Penny. 'Rod' was killed in a flying accident in 1942.

disliked Woody because, at Aden, Saul was his junior and Woody was the more successful with what females there were at Aden. At Newcastle, where Saul comes from, the WAAFs in the underground ops have to go about in threes, to be safe from their AOC. *(I met Woody again about eighteen months later at Gibraltar. He was in transit for Malta, waiting to be flown in or go in by submarine during the siege. He was to take post as Group Controller of Ops. We had a drink in the bar of the Bristol and again at the Rock, and I showed him round. I have never seen him since; but I heard that he was tired out by the time he was halfway through his tour at Malta; that he turned even more desperately to the bottle and that on this occasion he became a sick man and was sent home.)*

Dizzy back from four days leave in London which he spent in putting out incendiary bombs. Went with Rod to the Flint House where we joined Penny (his fiancée whom I know very well and before Rod met her; she is the blondest blonde I've ever seen and the prettiest). His view of marriage is largely founded on the desire to have a son by Penny, "whom I can teach to ride, shoot, fly, play games and so on."

Met Reggy and Eileen in Cambridge (pre-war Cambridge and Fleet Street friends). On return received very urgent from Browne at the Thriplow sick bay. A sapper had his head caught in the track of a tractor or a tank. I went up and was taken to theatre where Browne and an orderly were trying to clear his haemorrhage. It wasn't a pretty sight; he was unconscious; his skull was fractured and he seemed to have no face left. After half an hour of Browne's struggles, the poor fellow died; Browne turned to me and, waving his gloved hands, said, "It's your turn now, padre". He seemed surprised when I said, "It's too late for me, too." As we took off our things and washed, I asked what he expected me to do then and there: "Something, but God knows what. You ought to know." "I'll pray, but I shan't do it here and now." We talked about other things.

A "scramble" for a wing sweep while I was at WA1 this afternoon; very exciting; stayed for tea and waited for their return; had the usual gay time.

29ᵗʰ April 1941

On Sunday Rod brought Penny to Linton where she nursed Robert. They are a lovely couple and we all had a happy evening. Neither of them, when they are together, detracts from the other. Yesterday afternoon Dizzy and I looked at Rod's collection of photos. Alas, the really remarkable ones taken while he was at Ipswich Grammar School aren't here; he will bring them on his next leave. We then took mutual photos, each in turn wearing my collar.

Ian returned as a Flight lieutenant; rather embarrassed by it. Took him and Nigel to Linton where Nigel slept most of the evening, waking up to go home. He kept asking the day of the week and getting it wrong when he tried to remember.

1ˢᵗ May 1941

The RE's arranged for the sapper's funeral; they rang up the DACG at Newmarket and asked for a gun carriage; so a real cannon was sent to take the funeral. Funeral prevented me from going to the races (Thousand Guineas).

| *Patrick Bernard George 'Dizzy' Davies posing in Guy's collar.*

(The Mess had begun betting on a very heavy scale and I foresaw trouble ahead, particularly for the older officers who were betting more than they could afford to lose. I attempted with some success to control affairs by enlisting Ian's help: he produced a betting system, and this, with tips from a gentleman in Liverpool called "Source", enabled us to have a pool into which strictly limited bets were paid. The amount which each man laid was thus limited and the affair came under control; no one made any money except "Source" at Liverpool who charged a lot for his bad tips, but I think it was a useful if unorthodox piece of social service.)

Took Ted Smith to Magdalene to dine – dull evening and poor conversation. Leonard Haines was killed yesterday; he has been married six weeks. My new padre is extremely nice; he is an Oxford groupist but I have told him to shut up about this. He has agreed, and I think understands the reason for my ukase.

2nd May 1941

Michael Lyne and Harold "HO" Oxlin (19 Squadron) came home with me yesterday, generously bringing a crate of beer with them. We stopped at the dreadful Railway Tavern at Pampisford because it looks so frightful; it is as nasty as it looks; and over the bar in a bottle of spirits is a most revolting insect that must have fallen from a customer's head into the Ely beer and so perished. Back here, taking HO to WA1 at 2 a.m. without waking anyone up. Much talk about the bungalow which HO has built for himself at Snettisham. He and Michael get on very well with each other. HO is entirely new to operations.

Long talk with Vass this morning in his office. He asked me how he was getting on as CO; I replied that that was the one question a good CO didn't want to ask anyone. He got a bit ruffled and meanderingly explained what he was trying to do on the station, and why he had done what he had. I liked him the better for all this, but it is a very juvenile way of talking. I hinted as much and said the one thing any CO could never do, was to ask anyone how he was getting on; his responsibility so far as the station was concerned was final and couldn't be shared. It was different if his officers came and told him what they thought, so far as KR and ACI allowed; all this new to him and he seemed surprised and said, "But you aren't a regular, are you?" So I pointed proudly to my VR badges and replied that the onlooker from outside sees a lot of the game. Much more talk, for I had to say everything three times very simply before he could understand. He is good and simple, and I also explained gently that if he interfered again with my arrangements for Sunday services (he covered the altar in the hangar with the R.A.F. ensign last Sunday) I should be as good as my threat and leave him to take the service. However, I would gladly take the services I organised: I had been trained etc. etc. I wouldn't attempt to interfere with his operational orders in the Ops room. What would he think etc. etc.? He gradually saw the light. But I rubbed it home by saying that, if there were any more interferences such as that of last Sunday, he must take the service and I would gladly stay and worship. He thought I wasn't being serious at first, but I told him I was; and I added some nice bits about how much I valued his example and so on (which I do). We parted very good friends and with a degree of trust on my part which didn't exist before.

Big wing operation planned for today but was cancelled on account of weather over the south coast. Brilliantly fine here; squash with Rod after tea. Wing Commander Corner to lunch and long talk with him about 66 Squadron.

(Corner was an extraordinary officer. He was a doctor who had qualified as a pilot and became an operational one in order to observe the stresses on himself. Very little of this came out in our conversation. A little later on he was killed in a flying accident; he was the pilot and overstressed himself probably.)

5th May 1941

Yesterday was the first real summer's day. Blue of sky and hardly any wind. Parade service in the morning (with no trouble from the CO this time). Flew with Peel in a long-nosed Blenheim to Wittering in the afternoon. Wittering is a small and bumpy field and we landed fast right across the Great North Road. Went home on the bike in the evening and had more sensation of speed than in the air. Returned at 8 p.m. to find all on foot for a night patrol. Stayed up. We lost one fighter, a lad in 257 Squadron who couldn't land at Coltishall because it was being bombed. He crashed in flames at Ickleton, having just failed to get back here on empty tanks.

11th May 1941

On leave at home and having the happiest days, doing nothing except being with Thel and Robert. It is fine every day – Dunkirk weather – but too cold to sit out. We've had visitors by air and road. By air came Ian in a C40 and Rod in a Hurricane. Ian did some dives in his whizzer and some hovers which were not very comfortable to be underneath, for his engine sounded as if it was about to cut. Rod came over the next day at 5.30 p.m. and did some aerobatics from 8000 to 500 feet. A lovely display including some flying upside down across the garden. He also did the nearest thing to a flat spin without going into a tail slide. I asked him a fortnight ago if in theory it was possible to spin an aircraft straight and level, with the engine stalled. Now I know. He did about three or four. He told me it felt awful and he came out of it quickly.

Nigel and Ian came on Tuesday: Ian planning Marx Bros in Shakespearian films, and Marx Bros repertory season of Shakespeare at the Golder Green Empire. He gave birth to the good phrase "We labour to impress". The day before Rod and Penny came for supper; both gave us the happy evening to which we had been looking forward. They are a delightful pair and seem to like coming. Penny is as nice as she looks. They can't make up their minds about getting married. It's complicated – Rod's tenure of life is uncertain, though surely the time is coming when he will be posted non-operational. He told me we reckon German losses to be about 10 per cent, I had thought their raids were about 500 strong; apparently they are only 200.

Michael Lyne has been posted to Speke where he will remain for only a few days. Then he goes to a very wet job in Hurricane 1's. To be shot down seems to be the least risk. One is resentful that Michael should be sent on this enterprise. He is intelligent beyond the average, and as a Regular would be marked down for real leadership in the service. So away he goes. One prays he won't get killed – by shooting down, drowning or strangulation. He has always been a gay companion bubbling with conversation and I got to know him after he was wounded. I always looked forward to finding him at B flight dispersal hut, sitting over the telephone waiting to say "Scramble" or talking in the hut during fighter nights or here at the cottage with HO. The last two times I saw him were pleasant; we met by chance in Boots in Cambridge and we went to buy two very big cigars at Colin Lunn's. The other time was more recent: last Monday evening at WA1 in the Mess. It was a fighter night. It was after 10 p.m. and the lights were out; the only light was a hurricane lamp and the glow from the stove. The pilots at readiness, Lane, HO, Vokes and Michael were sitting round the stove, Michael wearing dark glasses. We talked in a desultory way and Michael was more than usually mordant in his remarks. About 3 a.m. all was called off and we went to bed. Now that he goes, only Lane is left of the original 19 Squadron pilots I first knew (and there have been four or more replacements of pilots since Dunkirk). So till the next meeting.

(Michael went to be pilot of a rocket-fired Hurricane, to be launched off a merchant vessel in Atlantic convoys to look for submarines. I met him at Gibraltar and saw a demonstration of the method of rocket launching from the foredeck of a merchant vessel. He got the DFC. We met again in Cairo when he had become a Wing Commander.)

15ᵗʰ May 1941

Returned from leave after a superlative seven days, including a memorable game of chess with Thel under the apple tree. Found that Duxford was bombed on Saturday: 12 bombs but they didn't go off – they were dropped much too low. Went to Newmarket for the races with Thel, on the July course. Cold but lovely with the cloud in massive formations over the Fens. The bookies looked a trifle thinner than usual. Between us we won about 45s.

Rod and Dizzy are busy writing reams of very bad poetry.

23ʳᵈ May 1941

Dizzy and Latimer shot down a Heinkel on Friday; they were over France when they did it. It was a gross piece of poaching for they were meant to be "local flying" only and deliberately maintained radio silence in order to go over the French coast.

(Chiefy Tuck, commonly known to himself as The Champ, was the Commander of the Duxford wing at this time. He was elegant in the extreme, with a slight lisp. Smoked cigarettes through a very long holder. On fine days he would like to stand on the steps of the Mess looking at the weather over the hangar tops; elegantly he would flick the ash off the cigarette and remark to me: "Too fine to stay here, Padre; I think I'll go over to Calais and get one. Ask them to keep lunch." For many days he returned successful; but during the summer the Germans were waiting for him and he was shot down and taken POW.)

Chiefy Lane is posted and is to have a rest from Ops. So goes the last of the original 19 Squadron pilots. Had a long talk with him this afternoon at WA1.

A typical day: I cleared up a mountain of paper work and letters this morning; spent a long afternoon at WA1 and returned to find a similar-sized mountain waiting for me.

WAAF dance last night. Penny has an embarrassing way of saying "I love you". Dizzy was here with his girl; I expected a blonde bombshell but she was a mouse. Have spent a long time this week with Rod and Dizzy for they are going to be posted soon. How dull and drab the Mess will again be without them. Been feeling lousy with catarrh; bags of phlegm. The new WAAF CO has red hair and looks a real "good woman".

28*th* May 1941

King George has lent me a grand new motor bike (a huge Norton). I went on it yesterday and felt frightened to death and thrilled. Went to Caxton on it today and loved it; got the real thrill of going fast on a motor bike with lots of power in reserve. The fields were yellow with buttercups, and the chestnuts along the Old North Road were just coming out. I sang hard and had the words forced back down my throat by the wind. Had some wonderful long bursts at 65 and a good bit over.

Peter and Bob killed just about a year ago today. 19 Squadron are roaring over, going on a sweep as I write.

2nd June 1941

Very depressed due to the weather which is as dull and cold as March. As causes for depression never come singly, the news arrived that Rod has been posted to Kirton where he will command a flight and later an army co-op squadron. Craster leaves for Wittering as a senior Intelligence Officer; so another source of private jokes and a companion for subtle games of chess disappears.

Robert's broken rattle has gone to Dizzy; I gave it to him last night. He wrapped it up in a boot box and I took it down to Ops room to give to Penny. She wasn't there. Controlled Dizzy for a short time from Ops and reported the safe arrival of the rattle.

5th June 1941

Rod left yesterday. Gave a farewell party the night before; 48 glasses were broken so I suppose it was a good party. The Mess is dull now. Heavy feeling hanging over everyone, for the outlook is very, very grim; even Dizzy is down and can't see victory on the very distant horizon. Budd and the "Giant Panda" in the same mood too, and me; but I've got to try and keep spirits up.

Went to the Q site on the Norton; called at home for a few minutes; had tea with Thel who is wonderfully cheerful. Robert was roaring with laughter all the time in his pram in the porch.

12th June 1941

Returned from a wonderful 48 hours. Arrived in time for tea to find Robert at the gate in his pram, ready to burst into laughter. Spent the evening at home; lounged about the next day; Thel working very hard.

Went to Cambridge via Duxford to pick up my camp bed; meant to meet HO at the Volunteer but the arrangements went wrong. Only at Trumpington did we think of ringing up Linton to find he was at the Black Lion. Raced back to fetch him and watched him eat. Got back home after 10 p.m. Thel awfully tired and went to bed at 2 a.m. HO and I sat up talking; he was asking why I was a Christian and so on: "I would like to know because I'm so fond of you both and I'm not one myself." So we talked till about 4 a.m. when we went down to the churchyard; it's a good place at that hour, with the ghostly cow parsley on the graves, the yews, and the pleasant air of neglect. We climbed on to the nave roof by a ladder which we put up. It was just beginning to dawn. A bomb dropped a long way off. The "all clear" went; you could see another dawn coming up and in the silence hear the cocks crow, calling out to each other that another day had started. We came down, visited the river and went to bed.

HO didn't wake up till about noon. I had breakfast outside and talked to Robert who is the soul of happiness. A little beer before lunch; talks with Thel; then down to the river. Tea with hot tea cakes; and so sadly, very sadly, returned here with HO. We are both fond of him. And he of us; at least he seemed to make that clear in the conversation. He seemed so grateful for hospitality that I had to make it clear that we weren't being kind but enjoying ourselves.

Party in the Mess on Monday – a mild one. Vass was flapping about and said sharply to Dizzy, "But you aren't released yet from readiness". (It was "birds walking weather" outside). Dizzy was standing in front of a table covered with beer glasses and doing valiantly with them. He paused in his busy work and said to Vass, "Then they'd better hurry up and release us". In the circumstances it became one of the remarks that won the Empire, though it sounds tame now. The atmosphere was electric. Rod was there, having flown over to see Penny, and he dropped a bit of chewed beef gristle in Vass's hat (which I removed in the nick of time). Tommy came with him; both have gone.

Damn: I'm getting fond of another fighter pilot (HO). It's dangerous but it would be wrong to have reservations with one's affections for fear of being hurt; as hurt we surely all will be before the summer is out.

13th June 1941

Report about Peter Howard Williams' death is wrong; I had a signal from Catley at lbsley. Played HO at squash and beat him. Today's saying – "I've got money to burn but I don't like the smell."

15th June 1941

The events of Friday make it a memorable week. After supper HO and I went to the William IV at Heydon; we played darts. It is a good rough pub with white scrubbed wood and a stone floor. HO was in the mood when he made unpredictable remarks. He joined in the local conversation about the bombing of the village (which he had only just heard about) saying, "Oh yes, I saw that one fall' and so on. I hadn't seen the bombing; he hadn't been on the station then. Conversation very difficult because it became general and I had to be careful not to say anything that would make us appear liars. That part of the evening was gay, comfortable and liquid. It was a fine summer evening, a high sky and no wind.

After that, we went to the Flint House which we left at 10.45 p.m.; beer and darts against an Air Ministry official. We stopped at secret Battle HQ on the way back and rather informally inaugurated them. I lifted the scrambler phone and found I was on a direct tie line to Ops room at Fighter HQ, so I put it down quickly.

I thought the evening was over; went to my room and started talking earnestly to the new chaplain, Spurgin, with difficulty for I wasn't feeling in an earnest mood. There was a commotion in the hall; the door was flung open and in came HO with a case of beer on his head. Poor Spurgin looked "shook" and went to bed shortly afterwards. We drank some of the beer with Nigel and went to bed at 1.30 a.m. HO was saying on Wednesday as we walked home from the church, "There's no reason why you should be so kind to me; I've done nothing and it makes me feel a sham". So I explained that we weren't being good or kind.

Robert busy cutting a tooth on Saturday; another lovely afternoon with Thel.

16ᵗʰ June 1941

Parade service at WA1 this morning. A sunny day. Went to Sawston to collect information about the crimes of Sergeant Irwin. Had tea at WA1. Afterwards, HO, Milman and I sprawled in the grass, sunbathing, near the shelter trench which overlooks the plain; we discussed infinity, eternity, atomic theory, entropy and the effect of shaking all the words of Shakespeare's plays in a box – how often would they fall out in the right order?

Before Milman came, HO was talking about how fine days should be spent and said sadly, "These days make me long for the time when I shan't have to fly." More talk by him about Friday evening and how happy he had been.

Rod came over yesterday; went up with him in his Blenheim. Had a very uncomfortable and enjoyable time in the rear gunner's turret. And I wasn't wearing a "parasuit" so my parachute didn't fit the tiny stool; I couldn't strap myself in. Part of the Perspex was open so I was in a surging gale. At least it gave a sensation of speed. We flew through the cloud base into clear sky and explored the cloud valleys and mountains, diving into valleys and going through the mountains; and then banking steeply to look at the earth through the holes in the cloud base.

We came down over the coast at Orford Ness, flew over Felixstowe, kept interestingly near the Harwich naval base and the balloons, and then made a swoop over the village where Rod was born. We beat up his house in Ipswich, a real beat up with the wing tip cutting the daisies, or almost, in the public park. Back home, turning very sharply over the Red Lion to visit Linton and so here with a very bad landing. Learned that Rod has only done four hours in Blenheims. He flew this one very light-heartedly; and when you looked back along the tunnel of the fuselage you could see his chestnut-coloured head in the pilot's seat, bobbing about, pointing out this landmark and that. After an orangeade he flew back to Kirton. The last sight of him was climbing into his seat and giving that curious circular wave of the hand in front of his face.

17ᵗʰ June 1941

Another scorching day, far hotter than yesterday. I sunbathed outside the "Vicarage", as I used to last year till I lost heart. I made a catalogue of virtues: Bob's fine manners and devotion to his mother, and his gentleness; Peter's energy and sense of duty, courage and tough loyalty; Michael Lyne's sensibility, liveliness and intelligence; Rod's strict code of right and wrong and his gaiety that comes from this discipline; Ian's gaiety of a different kind and intelligence; HO's interest in people rather than things, his candour, directness and happiness; and Dizzy's Elizabethan gusto.

Had a sherry party last night in the Mess for Chiefy Lane who left this morning. I was out of love with life and rather spoiled it for Thel. It was a quiet affair till 19 Squadron who had been doing a sweep over the Channel came in. Vass insisted on rushing to the window and counting the aircraft to see if there had been any casualties; he managed to knock most of the spirit out of the party even after 19 Squadron joined us. Ian ate an iris root and got a very sore throat. Curious to see HO suddenly change from his quiet, gentle self into a tough, and carry Chiefy round the room. Later Dutton, the new CO, was carried round. He will have to work hard to make himself good enough to replace Chiefy.

Went with Thel and Elizabeth to the Newmarket Derby. A terrific traffic block and an immense crowd made it all very uncomfortable, but we enjoyed ourselves; I only got one winner – Rue de la Paix. Back to Linton and Robert. Thel told me how grim the party was, not knowing how long the people you talk to are going to live e.g. HO planning to spend his half day with us on Friday. You plan it, look forward to it, and all the time is the thought – will he be alive then?

20ᵗʰ June 1941

Must be hot – I don't feel like squash. Arranged with HO for a half day at Linton but it had to be postponed; all were put to readiness at the last moment; and I had to stay in case I was wanted. President

Benes of Czechoslovakia and Sholto Douglas came to the station (as if there wasn't enough to do without them and "the bull"). Glad to have a sight of Benes. However, I wasn't wanted in the end so went to Cambridge to visit an unmarried, expectant mother; one of the Czechs is the father. It's a dismal story: he has a wife; the girl is alone and can't or won't tell her people who live in the north. I made some financial arrangements and saw to other details. It was a splendid ride on the Norton in the heat, but I must be careful – there was too much split-arse on the way back.

23rd June 1941

Had a half day yesterday. Took HO home; the sliding roof blew off on the way but we put it in the back seat. Bathed and sunbathed in the river for two hours, with gentle, inquiring theological discussion. In between times we chased trout without success; the water was cold, though on the bank the sun made the air very hot. We talked about having a mind trained to use leisure, and the disciplined use of leisure; and the discipline in every human relationship which is essential for its preservation; this was particularly concerned with HO's girl, and he made all the going in the discussion, not me. There was the contrast of the mind trained for some technical purpose and the failure of its special disciplines to be applicable to human relationships. HO kept saying, apropos of the occasional bathes and trout chases, how happy he was. We came back to the cottage for tea under the pear tree. HO won a triumph with Robert in picking him up and throwing him around. Robert burst into anguished tears when an exhausted HO put him down.

We went to four pubs for beer; HO in his dangerous, affable mood – talkative on any subject to complete strangers and chatty most on subjects about which he knew little. In one pub he was asked the classic "What does it feel like to fly? I see you up there and I say, 'There go the buggers again', meaning no disrespect, sir." The answer proved to be a very modest one, but I was frightened lest I should be called upon to support a most terrible "line shoot" so near to the ridiculous as to be a transparent caricature, or a work of pure fantasy and imagination, breath-taking in its unrealism. We listened to the P.M.'s speech on Russia, at home; we were beaten at darts in the Swan. We returned to Duxford about 10 p.m., where we talked in my room for another three hours, at the end of which HO went "to bed early as there may be a sweep in the morning".

Yesterday was one of the distinguished happy days that stand out in relief from among the other happy but less notable happy days. I tremble for his future and for that of the squadron. I take such a joy in friendship, in knowing people well, in trying to be known, in getting fond of people, and looking forward; and overall hangs this shadow – will they be here for the next time?

When we got back last night HO talked about dying, about having as much experience of life as possible before dying, and in just such a vein Peter used to talk, only HO can communicate himself better, and not surprisingly for he has the university training which Peter hadn't. And with HO there is the conception of having a full experience with the so-called limitations of discipline which preserve the experience and give it shape.

24th June 1941

Heat very oppressive, making me feel sick and floppy. I lay down this afternoon and then played squash with Ian as a desperate and successful remedy.

19 Squadron went to Malling and are doing another sweep over France, this time at 8 p.m. Shall go up to WA1 in case they come back tonight. Ian flew me to Kirton in Lindsey yesterday in his auto-whizzer; we generously consented to give the observer corps a plotting exercise so took an indirect route: here to Sutton Bridge, then over the Wash where we came down low and chased wild duck as water level. We kept pace with two, so they can fly at between 60–70 mph. We are thinking of going again with a gun. We would catch them in a net when they were shot. The Wash looked mysterious and eerie today and especially so, for there was a heat haze which made visibility very short. There

were queer deserted rivers; odd little tramp steamers doing nothing. We startled one bather on a mud flat miles from land. I hope he got back. We flew past Boston Stump and so across Lincs till we were in sight of Scunthorpe and then landed at Kirton. I did my business, which was to find out the details of a steam clothes pressing machine they have. Met Tommy Tucker who had come in his Spitfire from WA1. Left about 6 p.m. and returned via Lincoln and Peterborough, a real cathedral crawl; very enjoyable though the flying is very slow in an auto-whizzer.

Had a quick supper and then went to the cottage and sat in the garden till the midges drove us all indoors. Talk about a racing system.

310 Squadron go to Martlesham on Thursday, so we lose Dizzy, but the heat is something of an anaesthetic. Two corporals from MT have set to work on the body of the Hillman which was about to fall to pieces.

25th June 1941

Still feeling pretty limp; restless night wondering what had happened to 19 Squadron for they had to make an unpleasant landing at WA1 after dark. Went with "Wattie" first thing to WA1 and found them finishing breakfast in various stages of undress.

(Wattie's nickname was deliberate to distinguish him from Peter. He had been a stock broker but was now a sector controller in the operations room. He did not read much, but he was good at judging people. I relied on him and, looking back, I probably took more from him than ever I gave out to him. Our common interest was Peter whom we thought an exceptional pilot whose life must somehow be saved despite himself.)

We sat in deck chairs and they talked to us about the sweep – "they" being HO, Arthur, Tommy and Cowley. HO described very exactly what it felt like to have pink plumes of flak under your tail over France. Visited our men in Ely Hospital this afternoon. Sunbathed here on return.

Four brews of beer are common in these parts; to east and west, Greene King, Fordham and Lacon; to the west, these plus Royston Ales. Greene King though it varies from house to house is the best.

Fordham is always good; and Royston is the best within easy reach of the camp. At Linton there is a Benskin house, but the beer is never as good as at other Benskin houses in East Anglia. Lacon makes the change and should be tried when the opportunity offers.

Song for Male Voices (from R.A.F. Quarterly, June 1941)

> *The nectar which the gods distil*
> *Is more refined than beer.*
> *The latter has a vulgar touch,*
> *But sad to say my nature's such*
> *That I enjoy it very much.*
> *The same again, old dear.*

26th June 1941

Vass is posted to Air Ministry, to our ill-disguised relief. He really has no conception of what a CO should be like on an operational station; at one moment he is a frivolous hippopotamus, at the next a distressed and prudish grandmother. Macdonald, the new Wing/Co Flying, will command; so we are pleased. He is dour but he can be melted; and he isn't subject to violent changes of mood; and he has flown a lot operationally; Vass had never flown operationally, let alone led a sweep.

29th June 1941

Wattie and I went to WA1 for an evening with the boys, the boys being mainly Farmer, Jock, HO, Tommy and Denis Cowley. We had a gay evening just talking; I arranged with HO for another half day but this was cancelled as someone's dog bit his hand after we left.

Went home for the half day. I was feeling down with apprehension about the future of 19 Squadron; Thel cheered me up tremendously. At least last summer one didn't know quite what to expect; one only feared it. Now one knows and waits. 19 Squadron have been on sweeps every day for the past week. Got back to hear that Andrews was missing; Harkus (the O.D. Padre) had been to see his wife at Duxford village.

It was clear by yesterday morning that Denis Cowley was also missing. His wife is to have a baby in seven weeks' time; I decided that I had better go and see her. To my surprise, HO at once asked if he might come too. I agreed, being only too pleased to have a companion for this sort of journey. We left for Bedford after lunch, HO at the wheel. We had a long, tasteless and amusing conversation on methods of how not to break the news we were bearing. I couldn't trace Mrs Cowley in Bedford but eventually got her on the phone through some friends. Then called for HO who was at a Howard Hostel finding out how it was run; had tea there and learned what to do about buggery and bed wetting. Back here with HO navigating fairly well (there were no sign posts) and on to the cottage for supper. Michael Williams (Robert's godfather) was there with his "goil". HO attempted to display his bandaged hand in the pub as a war wound but efforts were entirely unsuccessful to enlist interest for the great British public know that pilots never talk about themselves. One Welshman showed some interest and HO was hopeful that here was a chance; but the Welsh man merely said that "airmen" should be tough anyway in tough times and that coalminers have a far worse time. Very disappointing.

30th June 1941

My afternoon sunbathe disturbed by Harkus, Nigel and HO; so no solitude or thoughts. I came over to the office and wrote letters to next of kin; a full evening service; cut the Sergeants Mess social and went with HO to the Trumpington Unicorn for cider – only a very little. We talked about Belloc and Chesterton and what beer meant to them and more seriously again about the full life in a short time. At the Grantchester Red Lion the landlady asked about Thel and Robert. Again we sat in the garden overlooking Cambridge. We went to the Rose and Star where the landlord's son, who is a bomber pilot in Manchesters, told us that civilian bombing didn't break morale, only made the people more sullen and determined.

At Shelford we decided to go back via Thriplow; on the way you pass the monument on the hill which I often see from the air and wonder what it is all about. So we climbed the hill, walked carefully across a wheat field. The sloping base to the monument is very steep and the inscription too worn to be read from the ground. So after many slips and falls, and after taking off our tunics and shoes, we crawled up and blessed one John Church who put the monument there, for some reason I don't remember, 200 years ago. The view was wonderful; there was a fiery red sunset lighting a cloudless sky; and the redness in the west beyond the low downs gave the illusion of looking hundreds of miles away. Over to the east you could see the water tower above Linton and more to the north were the spires and towards of Cambridge. Some Hurricanes leaving from Duxford were reminders that all was not as peaceful as the view.

We started off to the camp and, at HO's suggestion, exchanged tunics and collars and identity cards; so he became a squadron leader with my badges and I became an F/O with brevet. We were stopped in the dusk at the AA site, and young Battle, the CO, came out as we were challenged, and I asked leave to introduce the new padre who has just joined the service. It worked like a charm. Battle was most charming and restrained in his speech, not one "bugger" or "bloody" or worse. HO was realistically unctuous and said, "I hope to see you at our services at Duxford". Poor Battle got embarrassed and tried to explain that he didn't get much time to come down to the camp for services. Then HO and I burst the bubble by laughing. So he gave us a pint of beer and we went on to Duxford pickets. The guard was very impressed when HO said, "Station Chaplain here and F/O Oxlin", and to give them a chance of checking on the identity cards, he asked them the time in a very ecclesiastical voice, reeking with benediction. And so to bed but laughed for a long time before going to sleep.

Did Ulysses and his like ever really *"drink delight of battle"*?

1st July 1941

Went home for lunch. Robert looked more enchanting than ever, and I loved them both. Good to be home even for this scrappy visit.

HO's hand is healed again so he has returned to flying. Went to an
ENSA concert with Farmer, Jock, Tommy and HO but didn't feel very
ready to laugh with them. Will the uncertainty be ended tomorrow
afternoon, the day after, or when? Afterwards HO came over to collect
"Jew Suss" in German (but why had I got it? I don't know German).
Went through Denis Cowley's kit this afternoon; Joe Harkus went
through Anderson's.

2nd July 1941

Went to Newmarket with Ian; Thel couldn't go as her mother is still
away. Didn't seem like Newmarket without her. £1 of my winnings
fell out of my note case and was lost. A horse was shot on the course,
but from the fuss you would think they were shooting a trainer's
wife. Had tea at the cottage and Robert smiled approvingly on us
all. Went to WA1 after supper and spent the evening with A flight.
Met a Welch Regt officer whose father is a parson and who earns his
living in peace time by selling cars to the Church Pastoral Aid Society.
Tentatively arranged another half day with HO. He suggested that on
our annual leave we should spend some time canoeing on the Ouse;
he is to make an air reconnaissance of the river near Bedford. The
date must be uncertain though the intention is firm, the achievement
how indefinite! It doesn't do to make dates too far ahead, though it is
good for the other people's morale. Talked about Uffa Fox; HO went
off for night flying and I played shuv ha'penny and came back about
8.30 p.m. when night flying was over without any incidents.

7th July 1941

Went with "Fighter Boy Joe" Longbotham (*an aged but efficient
RAFVR who was commandant of WA1*) to WA1 for a social call.
Longbotham (and I) were disturbed to see that pilots who had been
released had not gone to bed; they knew that they would be flying on
a wing sweep at first light on Saturday. Fighter Boy and Farmer had

"words" but l kept out, thinking that I might more usefully interfere later and more privately. Left HO with my remaining ounce of tobacco.

Church parade has been washed out, for last night was another fighter night and everyone was either up and doing or lying awake and listening. Dutton has left 19 Squadron; has got a duodenal ulcer; Chiefy Tuck now commands the wing.

8ᵗʰ July 1941

The "buzzer boos" have come: I mean the largest, noisiest and clumsiest flying insects I have seen. Ian and I amused ourselves with killing them with squash racquets, and while doing this Norman Hill joined us and for no reason and quite suddenly debagged Ian. Rather odd.

Took a half day yesterday with HO; and it turned out to be one of those "not very often days" that stand out in relief.

It showed every sign of being cancelled in the morning but the Germans were thoughtful. We took a canoe on the Granta at Cambridge after lunch. At the town bathing station we saw Wattie and Ian so we bathed with them. We had changed out of uniform at the boat shed. After half an hour we went up towards Grantchester. I hadn't been up the river since I was "up"; and where the river runs into the meadows, we took everything out of the canoe and started swimming, and climbing in and out of the canoe, both at the same time. All this regardless of other users of the river who obviously thought we were maladjusted: out of eight attempts, we twice got in at the same time without upsetting the canoe, which had to be dragged to the bank and drained frequently. The water was right for all this; the day was the hottest we have had so far. After an hour of this and filled with Granta water, we paddled up to Grantchester and walked to the Red Lion for tea. The hot road was very painful to our bare feet. We paddled back to Cambridge in record time with a TERRIFIC thirst; never have I known one like it. The very kind of thirst that deserves Pimms No 1 and gets it at the Volunteer and again at the Bath. We changed to beer, had supper, and went to Trumpington but there was no cider: so we set out for Grantchester and at HO's suggestion took a look at Trumpington Church. I had forgotten it was so beautiful. We looked at Sir Roger (a very fine effigy of a crusader who came back) and Sir Roger looked at HO. I said nothing; I saw by HO's look that some idea of a common connection had sprung to his mind. There was no one else in church; it was getting dim; and I watched one "boisterous knight" looking thoughtfully at another one.

HO was annoyed by the verse near the tomb which reads:

> *Jesus Christ, have pity on*
> *Sir Roger, Knight of Trumpington.*

We talked a lot about this. HO resented the idea of pity; I tried to paraphrase, and he was surprised, I think, at the idea of God giving; so far he has thought of God demanding, as being of the essence of Christianity. I maintained, and he agreed, that there is nothing weak in asking God to have pity on us when we die, having tried to live fully and well; the pity is for the mistakes; it's not sympathy or condolence. HO said the incredible thing that knowing each other had for him made the Christian faith more reasonable and worthy of respect.

So we went to the Rose and Crown, the only pub in Grantchester which had any beer that night. We stopped at the mill pool on the way back; went through the woods, climbed the barbed wire above Byron's pool and bathed midway between the weir and the railway bridge. The moon came up – a full, ruddy fighters' moon; the water was very warm and the whole scene beautiful. The bathe was the more enjoyable for we had no trunks with us and there was no fear of outraging the decencies at midnight. HO started to swim down to Byron's pool, though I warned him that his lordship haunted it; and quoted lines and lines from Rupert Brooke's "Grantchester" which might have been written for this very evening. I followed him, but we both gave it up and, exhausted, lay on the bank. HO was so exhausted that he rolled into the river and was pulled out. We moon-bathed for a long time; watching a crowd of bombers going out across the moon to Germany. HO announced that he'd never climbed a tree naked; so he did. I preferred the bank; tree climbing with nothing on proved very painful and risky. But it got cold lying on our stomachs looking down on the water and at the moonlight catching the circles in the water made by the fish as they rose. HO lamented that so few people just lie and look at the light on the water and listen to the plosh of the fish as they rise, and talk. But it was getting cold near dawn, so we got dressed and returned to WA1, talking about God and the possibility (to HO) that He was manifest in natural beauty, and about experience as a test of validity in religion. I was glad he didn't turn to the problem of dying.

Some people were still up or had just got up at WA1 so we had sardine sandwiches and a little beer and I drove back to the camp blessing God. It was the kind of day that couldn't be foreseen and even hoped for; or any of its – or rather some of its – events hoped for or expected. Neither of us is inarticulate on any subject; as with Peter there are no reservations; as with Bob complete confidence and trust. HO is well-disciplined, I mean mentally especially. *Laus deo*. This morning I woke up with a very painful side as a result of the adventures with the canoe; HO won't climb trees again in the moonlight in unsuitable costume.

Some echo of last night sent me to the Old Testament and I couldn't think what l was looking for, till I realised after much thumbing that it was the mysterious incident of Jacob on Pennel *(which turned out to be the one of the Old Testament episodes which consoles Michael Lyne)*.

9th July 1941

Flew to Hendon yesterday in the Havoc; there and back within the hour; Jean Carriere was the pilot. I sat in the "arse end Charlie's" seat and enjoyed myself immensely; not so a Wing Commander whom we took with us; every time I looked back down the fuselage, I saw he was trying so hard not to be sick; we landed just in time; and he was sick when he got out; we saw him vomiting as we took off again and skimmed over the underground railway lines.

Spent the afternoon at WA1; there is little flying at Duxford now for the squadrons are dispersed to avoid destruction on the ground by bombing, and really Duxford is now an admin station and a dormitory;

and all our aircraft are on these secret fields round the countryside. Made a tentative day for next week with HO and went home to the cottage.

13ᵗʰ July 1941

Have spent a great deal of time at WA1 all this week, trying to iron out the difficulties about pilots not going to bed early enough when they are released, and trying to have the problem treated as a matter of common sense and not of service discipline, which will only put their backs up. Anyway, it's wonderfully cool up there on these sweltering evenings. Took Martineau, the new learner chaplain, up there on Thursday and let him loose while I had a long talk with HO and others about the anxieties which "Fighter Boy Joe" has. He thinks that several of the pilots are drinking far too much; it would hardly be surprising if you allow for the tension under which they are living. So I went to have a smell round and see what really was troubling the old man, for with all his goodness of heart he has a wonderful knack of making a complicated or personal matter not only formal and troublesome but also a matter of service discipline. I discovered that HO was high on the list of his suspects; and I found too that the old man had had his leg unmercifully pulled by several, including HO, who appeared, in order to shock the old man, to get "screeching" on the appearance of a crown cap opener. One, of course, is Arthur who, because he is very quiet, is all the more surprising as a leg-puller. So, without betraying confidences, I dropped some heavy hints, gave HO a bit of bull shitting and told him to pass it on to others and, after three hours, was able to return to Duxford and to pacify the old man who was really worked up.

Church parade here this morning in the hangar; a very good service, even though the lights went out in the middle; Macdonald, the new CO, comes, reads the lesson, is a communicant, but not a bible puncher, and doesn't interfere.

On Sunday mornings, it seems without end, I walk across the field at early dawn to celebrate communion in the chapel; there is a clear blue sky, with the threat of another scorching day; noises from the barrack blocks of the men getting up; and I say my prayers as I go; I can't pray for temporal welfare only; but for eternal and temporal welfare of the people on my "diptychs". Though a plea for their safety gets in; and for their safe return with honour (defend them in the heights). I suppose the simplest Christian prayer would be to commend them to God and his love. But it's not easy to be simple; there are some things that are bound to happen; and I don't want my prayers merely to be a safety valve; I do try to make them in line with God's will, which is their safety; even though He doesn't attach as much importance to the temporal part as I do. And I can't take the position that He must be on our side; war is wrong anyway; and, even though those who get caught up in it may start by having clean hands, they can't remain very long like that. It's all soiling in the end.

Have returned again and again to the story of wrestling Jacob and have now read all the commentaries I have on it; but of course the commentaries miss the point of the story as a type of spiritual experience of God and man. The point is often made that there is some identity between God and man in the common experience of suffering; but those who make the point don't expand it enough. They don't go on to say that suffering involves hanging on like grim death, hanging on to you know not what, with your eye-lids, rather than let go. "I will not let thee go, unless thou bless me." There are times when I think I must be agnostic about what I hang on to: except it's something more solid than I am, and immovable.

I suppose that; despite what I've written earlier, much of my prayers must be a safety valve; and if God is pity and mercy, why shouldn't they be? As long as they aren't becoming self-centred and a chat with God-in-my-pocket. I don't think there is too much risk of this and therefore of subjectivism, for so much of the prayer comes up as the result of allusion; in what one sees, hears, does; so that the actions of duty and service routine, the sight of familiar objects and the association of people with things, become the occasions for, as it were, a step to one side to let the light in and my own darkness out.

18th *July 1941*

Went home on 48 hours leave on Monday, spent mostly in the garden dealing with vegetables and in picking fruit for bottling; the charmer Robert directed operations from his pram. Came back very homesick. Cowley has turned up, wounded but picked up from the drink by the Germans.

Had a lovely flight last Sunday with Duckenfield in a Blenheim to Bascombe Down. Flew above cloud most of the way with patches of England showing through. Picked up "Banger" Rawlings and came back, staring at 6 p.m. The cloud had cleared; we could see the balloons over London; the gasometers at Harrow, 30 or 40 miles away, flew over West Wycombe and Reading and got back at 7.30 p.m. Very bad landing indeed coming back. Took Duckenfield on the carrier of my motor bike to WA1 in the evening. Just finishing my bath after squash yesterday when HO burst in very excited: Farmer commands the squadron; Arthur has got B flight.

22nd *July 1941*

Some odd instinct sent me to the Ops room last night; Wattie was controlling; and I looked at 19 Squadron plots on the board as they came back from a sweep over France. 19 landed at West Malling to refuel before returning here. A message came – we could see that there weren't the right number landing at West Malling – that Sergeant Brooks was missing; but it was clear also that there were two others missing. Wattie and I looked at each other, our hearts in our mouths; he went very white and I felt sick with foreboding. We didn't have to wait long; and Wattie, controlling his voice very well indeed, and giving me a warning look before he spoke, said: "Put up Oxlin and Tucker as missing." It was a terrible moment; there was no point in staying; I couldn't say anything to Wattie as he was much too busy controlling 19 who had left West Malling and were returning. So I went down to the teleprinter to have a word with Penny about Rod, and, weak all over and trembling, I went up to WA1 just as 19 were landing. There was little to add to what one had imagined: HO and Tommy were behind in leaving France, rather far behind, and couldn't catch up when the wing was withdrawn. They were seen to be shot down. Someone bailed out over the Channel and a launch has gone out. Came back numb and rang up Wattie and told him those few details.

Almost kinder if I hadn't told him, perhaps. But I reminded him that HO and I had breakfasted that very morning and that HO had told me that Wattie gave him more confidence as a sector controller than anyone else. We had also made plans for this afternoon, to be spent either on the river or in the university. But the sweep has put an end to that.

Went to bed numb, but woke up to find the numbness gone and desolation there instead. Must go and see his mother and sister at Stevenage; he came with me on the last of these news-breaking trips and we had that devastating conversation on how not to break news. Went to the Red Lion and saw Tommy's sister and told her. She was brave and already sensed that something had happened.

There is nothing more to say, since there's no one to say it to. Must wait for news. Thank God for what we have had together; the last half day was the one on the river in the canoe and the night bathe at Grantchester. And now I'm clutching to what we've done and talked about. So instead of having the afternoon with HO, I must go and see his mother and sister; in affection as well as in duty bound.

Does that make it harder or easier?

23rd July 1941

Yesterday was the bitterest day so far. Tommy's sister, after I had told her, went back to Mill Hill. I tried to work in the morning; in the afternoon I went in the station Humber (the squadron leader's pennant up, for HO would have liked that), taking Martineau with me so that he could talk on the way. It was a bitter journey; we left at the moment we should have left for the half day; and on the way bits of the conversation I had had with HO on the road to Bedford kept coming up. It was bitter, bitter, bitter.

I saw Mary and Mrs Oxlin; there was a moment of awful misunderstanding for Mary thought I had come en route for London; and I had to ask for Mrs Oxlin to come; she was resting upstairs. But they both smiled when I told them, and smiled when they asked questions. His mother said that as soon as HO joined she had got ready for this moment, so that he would have nothing to worry about; she wouldn't be his anxiety. Then she went on to say that, whatever had happened to him, he was still alive and developing – "becoming" was the word she used, whatever he was doing. HO would still be experiencing and living, and that was one of her fundamental beliefs. Mary isn't very like HO to look at; though every now and then there is a likeness and she has the same, rather rapid, jerky, interested manner of speaking which compels you to listen to whatever she is going to say.

I left them both still smiling: they waved to me from the door. I came away feeling that I had had news, almost good news, broken to me; I came away very small and humble at being bitter. On the way back I remembered what I had entirely forgotten in my self-pity – how HO had told me that when he went to Switzerland on his father's death, full of anxiety and unhappiness, on his first view of the villa where they lived, he saw that the flag was flying full mast as it only did for great and happy occasions and that his mother was waiting on the steps, happy and cheerful, to greet him. And she had said to him much what she had said to me.

I went to the cottage and told Thel. She told me that when HO last came to the cottage she had treated his dog bite rather lightly and laughed at it, not realising how painful it was. She told him she was sorry and wouldn't have laughed if she had known etc. And he had answered: "I hope you will always laugh about me, whatever happens; and, whatever happens, please think of me always as happy."

I have started to make the inventories of HO's and Tommy's things. It's the last and least thing I can do, and it is better that someone who knew them so well should do it. The summer has ended abruptly. But the sun is shining and the heat has returned, but no pleasure, no zest, except with Thelma and Robert. My own grief is nothing compared to the waste and suffering involved. There is really no hope for them; it is beyond doubt. So the shutter falls and there is silence; there was still a lot to say and to hope for. One thing I cherish and that is that evidently I was able to show him something of the reasonableness of Christianity and its truth. There wasn't time to say much really. I like to think of him standing beside Sir Roger, and I'm glad I persuaded him of the goodness of the prayer "Jesus Christ have pity on ..." So on HO.

28th July 1941

The last of HO's things have come from Malling; they were the contents of his pockets which he emptied before taking off.

Went to Q site; tea with Thel; Michael Williams turned up and so saw his godson again. He is doing his best to get transferred from the military police to R.A.F. aircrew. *(He succeeded and was lost off Beachy Head two years later)*. Both chaplains on leave; so am tied to the station. 19 Squadron away on another sweep. Monday's events are still heavy on me though I can't make any reference to them, except to Wattie. Celebrated communion yesterday for HO and Tommy and for their families. "Remember for good ..." HO repeatedly said that one good thing about the R.A.F. was that partings were sudden, unforeseen and never drawn out, "the effects of parting or death are both sharp."

7th August 1941

Played squash in Queen's with Michael Williams; went to Grantchester afterwards; was glad Michael was there for he helped to exorcise the memories of some of the places. Letter from HO's uncle today; sent all HO's letters to Mrs Oxlin by registered post, despite service regulations.

8th August 1941

19 Squadron were decoy wing over France yesterday; went up to WA1 to meet their return. Two missing: Bruce Milman and the Czech sergeant.

The Czech is almost certainly dead, shot down by flak; but, as we waited, we heard that Bruce is safe, having crash landed on Charing Hill in Kent and is now in Leeds Castle, critically ill.

Bruce alive this morning, but only just. Farmer is very angry and sullen about these casualties; wouldn't join in the general talk during which "the Champ" was describing to us what had happened, with all the gusto of someone who likes fighting. But I got Farmer talking by himself and got it all out: he is sure that these casualties – HO, Tommy and the later ones – are because 19 are being forced to use an old mark of Spitfire. Farmer bitter because, with other Spits, he is confident that the losses would have been avoidable.

10ᵗʰ August 1941

Bruce died late last night. 19 go to Coltishall this week; am going on 7 days leave so shan't be able to say goodbye. We are all sad at the move. I know not only the pilots but the airmen and NCOs so well; and I've watched and tried to look after them all since I came here. Been to their parties, buried their dead and sat and been a safety valve when they needed it.

Spent the evening with them in the Mess at WA1 before going on leave. Took a visiting officer with me; at the end, and not knowing all the facts or the record, he told me that he thought that in 19 Squadron there had been ever since the war the flower of the fighter pilots. There is a curious pride about them, not to be noticed in other squadrons and pilots in all kinds of tensions. They have the conviction that they are the best; it irks the others; but it infects everyone down to the cook. And you meet airmen who say proudly, "I was once with 19". HO told me that at Montrose the Irks used to say they had been with 19 as evidence of their efficiency. In their squadron log book is a quotation from Johnson which I wish I had copied; it is to the effect, "We attempt the impossible because it is harder."

I'll go on leave now. I can only think of them in terms of courage, kindness – especially to me – and gaiety.

18th August 1941

Just back from a strenuous seven days and gloriously happy in being home with Thel and Robert. Bill Seprell, a Canadian, visited us during the leave: he is a bomber pilot, quite unlike any fighter type; gave Thel a Benzedrine tablet but would have charmed her without that. He's now been killed. Sergeant Calvert is missing. Sergeant Lamb has shot himself in his bunk; there is some sinister story behind this shooting, and there is a hint that it wasn't suicide. MI5 have turned up in force.

Found, of course, that 19 have gone. Ichabod, Ichabod.

21st August 1941

Have flown with Rod in his new Lysander; went to Linton in it and did dives and flat turns over the cottage. I've always wanted to fly in a Lizzie; and now I have. Hooray!

27th August 1941

Took Tommy's car home yesterday. It's a 7 cylinder Alvis and the drive was fast and furious to Mill Hill. Had tea with his parents and Pauline. They are still hoping and have devised some fantastic theories to buoy up their hope. I tried very gently to hint that the time for hope was over. Grim seeing Tommy reflected so accurately in his parents and in Pauline. One's going seems to help.

Went on to Leicester Square; ordered new rain coat from Austin Reed. Walked to Waterloo and thence by bus to the Bank. Ragged Robin is growing in the ruins in the City; on the wall of Hungerford Bridge is a faded scrawl – "Long Live Moseley." The City looks a sad shambles. Had a gigantic and good dinner at the Liverpool Street Hotel. Very sad waiter who kept reminding me, as he recommended whitebait and grouse, that if you have the money you can always get good food. Letters from Mrs Oxlin and Mary; HO is posted as missing, believed killed. I think he's found "in evening light the decent inn of death", to quote of HO what he used to quote to me over a blue mug of cider.

29th *August 1941*

Went home last night – lovely, lovely, lovely. How I wish now I was home.

News has come that both Farmer and Jock are missing after yesterday's raid on Rotterdam. Farmer came down in the sea and was "pointed." Jock was last heard crying over the RT: "I can't make it; I can't make it." Six pilots from 19 Squadron went out this morning to search, but only two have come back, though not here, of course. So of all those who were with 19 last summer none are left, and none are left either of those who were here this June, 1941. The entity of the squadron has vanished. I'm glad that HO was shot down, if shot down he had to be, before he saw all his friends lost.

15th *September 1941*

Mary came to take HO's car away. It's an Austin 7 and had to be towed. We had tea in the Ladies Room and she talked gaily with those vivid echoes of HO in her voice and flashes of likeness across her face. I gave her his admiralty chart to take away, for it was his most prized possession.

Last Wednesday "Banger" Rawlings flew me to Driffield for 48 hours leave at Bridlington. Clouds were very low and we had to fly under them at about 400 feet all the way. We took a chance and crossed the Humber without getting any flak sent up; we landed at Driffield without doing a circuit, for Banger was in a hurry to get to Catterick. After asking the duty pilot about buses, I raced from the station on foot to Driffield; I noticed two air officers behind the watch tower, noted bags of gold and scrambled egg all over them; so I threw up a fine salute and still hurried on. I heard on my return to Duxford that one was the AOC-in-C of Bomber Command who promptly interviewed Banger about landing without doing a circuit. Banger offered profuse apologies, but the AOC-in-C turned them aside and wanted details of the "priest" who had "run like a rabbit from our Blenheim". Why hadn't he waited to see me and so on? The duty pilot explained about the bus service, and the war was then resumed in a normal way.

Got to White Stacks at 2 p.m. having taken longer in the bus than in the Blenheim. Shopped with mother in Scarborough; and returned here by rail via York on Thursday; mother and father looking well, despite noisy nights. Felt happier about them now that I had seen them for myself.

29ᵗʰ *September 1941*

I am keeping the diary only sporadically for what there is to record is not exciting, though the days are full enough of work and there's not enough time for going home. With the departure of 19 Squadron we face the fact that we are no longer in the van of fighter stations. Direct touch with the war has receded, and most of the operational squadrons are now further south or nearer the coast. Odds and ends of units arrive here; there is a Fleet Air Arm unit, with some good types in it, who will pretend that they are at sea; they "come aboard"; the ratings take off their hats when they come into my office. There is port and starboard to be reckoned with. AFDU is still here, bigger than ever. The American volunteer fighter squadron is forming here, the Eagle squadron. The pilots are very quiet, wealthy by our standards, rather over-awed by even the simple customs of this Mess, and well-mannered. I've moved from the "Vicarage" which has been renamed "the Manse" since Joe Harkus remains there. And I am in a large double room at the front of the west wing of the Mess. It's more convenient; I needn't live in suitcases; it has running water. It's nearer to everything, and it's noisier.

Came back from 24 hours leave to find two Eagle squadron corpses awaiting disposal, Barrel and Soarer; I knew them by sight only. They collided in landing at WA1.

This is an autumn of discontent; the leaves go from the trees; and one's friends in the Mess have gone or almost all of them. Summer seems a long way away and its times almost unbelievable. The King has given me a new motor bike, a 500 cc BSA, a grand animal.

7*th* October 1941

Went to Babraham signals and talked to the crew whom I now know best among the men on the station. Had a long talk with an airman from Bath called Oliver about Eugene O'Neill. Rashly I dared him to bathe; he accepted it; so we went to a very cold stream, with no witnesses and bathed rapidly. Stayed to tea.

9*th* October 1941

A black day for us all here. We weren't feeling very gay with the news from Russia; the Germans are 150 miles from Moscow and the Russians are still retreating. Even Joe Harkus speaks of us as being a decadent nation and foretells woe. The weather is wet, and we aren't yet used to the early blackout. Lord Haw Haw gave Tommy's name among those killed, in his broadcast last night. So I imagine that HO came down in the Channel; I hope he was killed first. In a way I'm glad he didn't survive to see what is happening now.

Our immediate bleakness comes from 133 Squadron which has been here temporarily. They left for Eglington yesterday; they flew to Sealand and refuelled. There the weather report was bad over the Isle of Man. Cloud 10/10 at 2000. Four were killed flying over Man: one bailed out over the sea and has been picked up; two flew into the mountain. Mann turned away in the cloud and spun in. The Group Captain sent for me and asked me to go and break the news to next of kin locally; I found one at the Red Lion, Whittlesford, and someone else came up here to see me later. She was very brave. She has been married five weeks and was bitter at the waste of life. But why are people bitter after the war has started?

It's been very trying; and Mac, the Group Captain, has been feeling it very much, the more so as the AOC on the telephone has been trying to fix the blame on Mac. I'm sorry for good George Brown, the CO; I know him well, for he used to be in 66 Squadron last year; from all accounts blame seems to rest with him, though he certainly is far from being a split arse pilot. He returns for a court of enquiry.

A corporal from 601 pay accounts has just come and burst into tears. I tried to put concrete into him; a lot of the trouble is due to the Oxford Group. He comes to see me again in a day or two. I have just reassured Mrs George Brown over the phone that George is safe.

Two men have got badly burnt at WA1. Went up. This is enough for a day, so went to bed before the next disaster, if any.

15ᵗʰ October 1941

Billy Burton came here today; he is now at Group HQ. I knew him quite well last year when 66 Squadron were operating from here. We examined a ME 109 which is here for research. The court of inquiry has cleared everyone except the pilots (of 133 Squadron) who were killed. Sir Paul Dukes came here to lecture about Russia; gave a favourable picture of the Red Army and this frightened the Tory diehards into thinking he must be a communist. Was appealed to, to try and reverse the effect of this propaganda by Dukes. Well! Well!

Letter today about a Wellington crash which happened some time ago. Mother of pilot who should have been flying wants a wreath placed on the actual pilot's grave; another letter from the pilot's wife telling him of the birth of a son. How was it that she has never been told? Not our responsibility here for the aircraft didn't belong to this station but just crashed near here.

22ⁿᵈ October 1941

Flanagan and Allen, the comedians, here for a concert. I gave them lunch in the Ladies Room; a very difficult meal indeed, for Hewlett was killed yesterday, and his mother arrived at the same time as Flanagan and Allen and wanted to see the body. Very difficult because really there is no body; and the coffin is filled mainly with sand. Kept having to leave lunch to keep in touch with the next of kin and the sick bay and to head them off from seeing the coffin. By much phoning and cooperation from the doctor, the coffin was screwed down quickly;

as soon as this was done, I took them over to the chapel and told them kindly that the coffin had been screwed down, and I was sure they wouldn't want it opened. Then back to lunch. Felt I must excuse this apparent rudeness to Flanagan and Allen, and so explained; wished I hadn't, though I didn't go into detail; for they became very upset indeed; however, we managed to restore them in time for the show.

Went to London on Tuesday for a conference at the *News Chronicle* with the editor, John Collins, and Bryan Green about some religious pamphlets. Spent too long in mooning over the ruins over the city; and felt very sad for Bob.

Went to the Caesarawitch at Newmarket with Thel and Ian. Very cold. Very bad luck for me, though not for Thel or Ian.

24th October 1941

Officiated at a pilot's funeral at Golders Green crematorium. He was killed through stunting in an Airacobra at Bedford. A party of us went in the station Humber, self at wheel driving very fast indeed. Extreme gloom naturally on the part of the pilots who came: I didn't want them to come. So gave them some port before the service. That cheered them up enough but not too much. It's all very urbane and slick, with synthetic sympathy and whispers of canned music at the crematorium. "Be Burned Slick." When the doors opened at the committal and the coffin disappeared, I saw a gentleman in a chef's hat and white coat, arms akimbo, looking at me. No one else could see him, fortunately; for a moment I wondered whether this was a glimpse of the "other side". The irony of it all is that it was Hewlett's funeral and cremation had already taken place in the aircraft. We zipped back along on the Great North Road, doing 70 most of the time; past HO's home and Tommy's.

29th October 1941

Rodwell, my library clerk, and I have tried to recondition the Hillman engine by squeezing a tube of "Overhaul" into the cylinders. Engine won't move at all. It cheered everyone up. When we got it to go, there was a terrible explosion, followed by clouds of revolting black smoke which obscured the car.

News today that Derek Graham has been killed flying in Scotland. His mother lives at Rievaulx, and I've written to her, for I knew him better than some and hoped to see more of him. He would have been the kind of young man who could have played a big part in reconstruction after the war. Behind his shy manner, which concealed a dislike of flying and fighting, he was brave; but his shyness and reserve suggested to some people conceit and laziness. He could be stubborn, but that was the worst you could say of him.

Long, long violent argument in the Mess till the small hours with the objectionable Preston (an officer of my own age). He may design good gun mountings, but he is poisonous. I got a bit hot when he told me that chaplains would be more useful in factories just now. At this point Ian and some others joined in and answered him more robustly than I cared to; one said, by way of concluding the whole matter, "Anyway, we all know you are mad and a bloody shit, Preston." Geoff; the naval adjutant of RNAFDU, and George Baldwin, the RC naval pilot, also joined in. George was very good at pounding away at Preston's infallible ignorance.

The Vicar of Duxford, who dislikes me, is a bit mad, too. He has suggested to the young corporal, Stanley Weber that he ought to be ordained. He doesn't know Stanley Weber.

Am training in the gym since there isn't much chance of regular squash; shall probably kill myself. Have made Rodwell train as well: told him he was getting soft, poor lad!

Snow and bitter cold. Joe Harkus is to go east in December: all very secret but we know it's Malta, even if he doesn't. I don't look forward to working with any other Nonconformist. When I take a united evening service, every other Sunday, I always try and make them as Nonconformist as I can; and now I discover that when Joe's turn comes, he takes Anglican evensong. I puzzled Joe by asking why we shouldn't just take it turn and turnabout and not bother about trying to be Nonconformist or Anglican; he didn't see this at all, so we will

go on. But I have explained to him, and I think he understands why, when he has a communion service, it can't be a "free for all".

All Souls Day 1941

Celebrated communion for my friends and all the others. Deck was killed in a Typhoon yesterday: he spun in near Thetford. All the Typhoons which are still experimental have been grounded. It is thought that he was gassed by carbon monoxide, as Ogilvie nearly was in the Airacobra. Peter Howard Williams turned up today, complete with DFC. A lot of exciting stories about shooting up trains in the Cherbourg Peninsula and much else about "Rhubarb". Told me that Leonard was killed through stunting near his wife's flat; his pupil was killed, too. Had seen Derek recently: he was killed night flying. Surprised that Peter thought so well of Derek: they are very unlike.

Peter looks cleaner than when he was with 19 Squadron and is as gay as ever; he brought back some of the vitality of March 1940.

4th November 1941

Went to London yesterday in my car to see Deck's next of kin at the Grosvenor. Arranged funeral with them. Took Rodwell with me to buy books for the station library. Went home in the evening. I am beginning to feel heavy and frayed and am getting jumpy. Want something more than leave, probably a posting: have been here too long. Though if I had the guts, this is the time when I should be learning to be most on top of myself. Rather lonely here; Ian and Nigel aren't here very often; the quality of the remainder isn't so good. Joe's posting is a knock; and the nearer it gets the more I feel it. Have got seven days leave next week. Hooray.

8th November 1941

Spent a happy afternoon with the signals at Babraham; but no more bathing; had tea with Ken, Freddie, Syd and the rest. Talk about John Gielgud, drama, lines in the newspapers and lots of standing jokes. Came belting back on the BSA in frosty air which made my head ache agreeably. Smoke lingered at tree height; the sun sitting red behind the hangars as I came up from the railway station. An exciting autumn afternoon. The Sergeants Mess came for a party last night. Hooked one Canadian Sergeant Pilot who is coming to see me for instruction. Odd card game during which all the players chanted "There goes the last of the fours" and so on. Long talk with the Intelligence Officer of 56 Squadron who is a recent convert to Rome. Another game involved drawing a pig in chalk on the table and rubbing out portions according to the shake of the dice.

Am still feeling very unsettled though there is lots to do, and with the recession of war from here, there is more and more personal instruction than I can very well manage. I seem to have lost temporarily my stability: annoyed by pin pricks which I would have ignored once. Thinking of asking for a posting: there are other operational stations near here. There seems nothing to be uneasy about but I am very uneasy inside and uncertain of myself. All the personal instruction is rather tiring, but it's worth it.

Buried Deck at Honnington on Thursday. Went with the "gay Giffy" who was in a very sombre mood indeed. It was a sad affair: the coffin was late in arriving; our silent wait was broken by women sobbing; and the tears showed on their furs. Deck's brother was upset. A very distressing service, and everything happened to make it more anguished than usual.

9*th* November 1941

A near gale blowing all day. One of my pupils made his first communion with the S.P. who suffers from alopecia. We had a good service at WA1; and here later I managed to make the nice but unruly Welch Regt sit up and listen.

Talked to Sergeant Innes and then did an hour in the gym. Talked to (Sergeant) LAC Layne in the cells. I saw him publicly reduced to the ranks in the barrack square on Friday after sentence of court martial. He refused to go to Malta because, as he said, there was a vendetta against him there among the Maltese; and he feared for his life. He made a scene at the humiliating ceremony, which should never have taken place as a parade. He still keeps his brevet; they couldn't take that away. He goes to the Glasshouse, and I talked about how he could "take" his sentence and about it not leaving a mark and so on. Perhaps I helped a bit there.

Spent the evening talking in the Church Army Hut.

17*th* November 1941

Returned from seven days leave – the mean King George narrows it to six days by my reckoning. Browne, the doctor, is going to Canada. So that is one of the old original Duxford boys less. Wise and energetic beyond duty for welfare: witness his example and mine when we ate an airman's supper after our own, publicly in the Airmen's Mess, just to show the food wasn't so awful!! He helped me a lot after a rather brisk encounter at the start: "Who is this bloody padre?" He sent me lots of difficult men and went a long way out of his way to help the ones I sent to him. He has humour and that helped a lot last summer and the one before. I liked his never-ending joke about the lack of dust on my trousers on Sunday, which I countered by pointing out the absence of blood on his cuffs.

A queer Irish padre has turned up, straight from some obscure cathedral in southern Ireland, very gauche, shy and frightened.

A wonderful leave at HOME. I can't write more: only repeat it. To come back here is like diving into a dirty, cold bath at the deep end and emerging in the warmth and light. Read Pepys on leave, the first time seriously.

22nd November 1941

Had our quarterly party last night. Thel came. Nice but dull. I went home with Thel afterwards: she makes me happy, happy, happy. Can't give any reason for my depression here but its continuance make me uneasy. Have been here too long. Why don't they move me without being asked? So much easier. Ian is here again; but even he is incredibly and surprisingly tiresome in the Mess; strong feeling that he ought to be operational and that he is running away from the war. *(All quite false in fact for his research, which was secret, was more dangerous than operational flying; he was jumping out of aircraft with a sort of autogyro fitted to his back.)*

601 Squadron are to lose their Airacobras and have Typhoons, for Airacobras only work well on runways. Going to bed at 8.30 p.m.

2nd December 1941

Signalled to go to the Air Ministry yesterday. An interview with Charles Gilmore which was like a scene from an adventure novel. He described a station to which he wanted me to go (i.e. I was going to be posted anyway); no name mentioned at first; told graphic details about threats of mutiny, bad senior officers, drink, immorality of both kinds (and several other kinds) rife; drunkenness abounding; and all the rest. And then he added in his smoothest, most novel-like voice: "And we think that operationally it's going to have the toughest of tough times soon. There's no chaplain there; one must go at once and get things sorted out from top to bottom before the thunder breaks there. Whoever goes will be directly responsible to the Air Ministry, not to the command." It was like a scene out of John Buchan, particularly the bit about being responsible to Air Ministry direct. I asked if I could be told where the aerodrome was which served both Cities of the Plain but Charles merely laughed and, continuing the novel-like scene, lit his pipe. It took a long time to light of course – it always does in novels. He then said how glad he was that I was going. (He knew this, of course, all the time.) I asked again but was told no more than it was overseas, and so it was secret. *(No one was told about where they were posted to overseas because of security risks with convoys.)* Could I go in 48 hours? I said, no, certainly I couldn't. "What a pity," Charles said. "There is a flying boat leaving from Plymouth in 48 hours and there is room on it." Otherwise it would mean going by convoy.

So I knew it was Gib and said so. I was right. I am to go by sea in about a fortnight's time. I hurried back to Duxford without waiting to hear any more, feeling frightened, very frightened indeed. I went straight home, without seeing anyone on the station, to tell Thel. That was very hard. It was very hard indeed, for young Robert was in his cot as we talked. Thel was very brave and more adorable than ever. I got back to the station at 8.30 p.m.

This morning I went to see Mac (the Group Captain) and told him privately. I asked for 48 hours leave which I got; but I knew that embarkation leave would follow this, so that I need never return to Duxford. I could settle up here without parties or farewells. I told Stevens, my clerk. He seemed very upset and said he didn't know what he would do. I told him that, as I didn't know about accounts but only pretended to, and, as the next chaplain would know nothing at all and wouldn't interfere, he could be happy. He is a good man. He saved me one awful night when I seemed to have lost £4,000 in the balance sheet. On another night he saved me when it took hours to trace a missing penny in £800. He was horrified when I suggested that I should make an anonymous donation of one penny to square matters and save time. I told Joe Harkus, the O.D. chaplain. He leaves next week for Malta (What price convoy security?). I saw Stanley Weber and told him that he was old enough to stand on his own feet. Air Ministry is posting my successor tomorrow, so he can tidy up the affair of Johnny Sale and Gaskell. I shall miss the vivacity of young Rodwell who has run the libraries so well. I told him I was going, since we have been more or less in confidential relation. I told him he needn't be afraid that my successor would try and kill him with exercise in the gym. All the same he seemed sad. So after an hour or so the whole thing was rounded off in a whirlwind of energy. I had dinner in the Mess but said nothing to anyone about my move.

After dinner I went into the anteroom and by happy chance it was entirely empty. I took up my usual sloppy stance, lolling against the high fireplace. I looked at the huge room and foolishly began to people it again with the living and the dead. I was looking on an empty stage. The cast had gone and could never be reassembled.

The room has been a place of bitter experience. But the scene to the mind's eye was gay. I remembered my first entry to a full anteroom with the occupants leaping to their feet out of respect for rank. That seemed a long time ago. I caught again the sombre undercurrents in my own mind which flowed beneath the chatter of pilots when the squadrons were fighting and you didn't know who would be in for lunch and who would be supping with God in Heaven. I didn't stay very long. I went to the chapel and then to my room to pack. I left after breakfast the next morning. I knew that I should never want to go back again. I had stayed there too long already. I felt as if I had been compelled to stay at a house after the guests had left and

> *After the bravest and the best*
> *Had said 'Goodnight'*
> *And gone upstairs to rest.*

Notes on the Text

As mentioned in the introduction, Guy was not infallible when it came to recording the names of the people he described. Some of the people Guy knew and worked with most closely, such as Peter Watson and Harold Oxlin, are discussed in great depth, and their life stories told in a great deal of detail, often including their tragic deaths. Others pass more fleetingly through Duxford – and the pages of Guy's diary – and often are mentioned only by nickname, part of their full names or with an odd erroneous spelling.

'Studd of 66', the 'drooping and bored figure' who Guy liked and whose death is recounted on 19 August 1940, was likely 22 year old John Studd. 'Griffiths', the No. 222 Squadron pilot whose death in a flying accident casts such a pall over the station and its officers in March and April 1940, is actually John Oliff Griffits. Poor 'Barrel and Soarer' from 29 September 1941 are American pilots Charles Barrell and Walter Soares. Guy's willingness to record as much as he could in the moment leads to these occasional confusions, making some of those to whom he refers difficult to trace, even with a wealth of other material now available. Sometimes, the name of a pilot must be inferred from these other sources. The No. 264 Squadron pilot whose body is found 'in the corn' on 11 June 1940 is almost certainly George Hutcheson, a 30 year old from Edinburgh.

Rather than break up the text with lengthy pieces of explanatory prose, identifying everyone or correcting odd spelling errors, we have largely left the diary 'as is'.

Sources for further research:

For readers interested in finding out more about others mentioned in Guy's diary, the Commonwealth War Graves Commission is a sad but vital source for information on the eventual fates of some of his friends: www.cwgc.org

RAF Operations Record Books (unit daily diaries, useful for corroborating dates) for the Second World War have now mostly been digitised and are available from the National Archives: www.nationalarchives.gov.uk

There are several interviews with Duxford personnel held by IWM, some of which can be accessed via the IWM website: www.iwm.org.uk

Kenneth Wynn's *Men of the Battle of Britain* contains biographical information on those pilots – surviving and fallen – who fought in the Battle, including Duxford's own.

Several books have been published about Duxford's Battle of Britain. Of these, 'Woody' Woodhall's *Soldier, Sailor and Airman Too* is particularly useful, as is Brian Lane's *Spitfire!*. Perhaps the accounts I find most moving are the Duxford chapters of Jim Bailey's *The Sky Suspended* and Tim Vigors' *Life's too Short to Cry*: their tone complements Guy's diary rather well.

Finally, a visit to Duxford will allow you to explore many of the locations Guy describes. It is fascinating to follow in his footsteps even though, as the diary attests, very few people could fill his shoes.

| Carl Warner